Economic Inequality in Latin America

Göttinger Studien zur Entwicklungsökonomik
Göttingen Studies in Development Economics

Herausgegeben von/ Edited by Hermann Sautter und/and Stephan Klasen

Bd./Vol. 37

PL ACADEMIC RESEARCH

Carlos Villalobos Barría

Economic Inequality in Latin America

Migration, Education and Structural Change

PL ACADEMIC RESEARCH

Bibliographic Information published by the Deutsche Nationalbibliothek
The Deutsche Nationalbibliothek lists this publication in the Deutsche Nationalbibliografie; detailed bibliographic data is available in the internet at http://dnb.d-nb.de.

Zugl.: Göttingen, Univ., Diss. 2012

Cover design: © Olaf Glöckler, Atelier Platen, Friedberg

Cover illustration by Rolf Schinke

Gratefully acknowledging financial support by Ibero-Amerika Institut für Wirtschaftsforschung and Verein der Freunde und Förderer des Ibero-Amerika-Instituts Göttingen.

Library of Congress Cataloging-in-Publication Data

Villalobos Barría, Carlos, 1980-
Economic inequality in Latin America : migration, education and structural change / Carlos Villalobos Barría.
pages cm. — (Göttingen Studies in Development Economics, ISSN 1439-3395 ; band/volume 27)
Includes bibliographical references.
ISBN 978-3-631-63976-4
1. Latin America—Economic conditions. 2. Latin America—Social conditions. 3. Equality—Latin America. I. Title.
HC125.V545 2013
305.5098—dc23

2013012571

D 7
ISSN 1439-3395
ISBN 978-3-631-63976-4

PL Academic Research is an Imprint of Peter Lang GmbH.

Peter Lang – Frankfurt am Main · Bern · Bruxelles · New York · Oxford · Warszawa · Wien

www.peterlang.de

Contents

Author's Preface

> "I have a dream that my four little children will one day live in a nation where they will not be judged by the colour of their skin but by the content of their character."
>
> Martin Luther King, Jr., August 28, 1963

Since I was a child, my parents instilled in me the idea that no one deserves to be poor, and that the opportunities are what makes the difference and that I should be very grateful for the situation I was born in. Now, many years later, I still have my parents advising from a distance and always reminding me that I must be grateful for the life I live and the opportunities that others have probably deserved more than me.

Apart from my parents, there is another person who marked me deeply when I was 13 and began to be aware of the world around me. This friend I speak of is called Germán, who was at the time a boy of my age whose family was poor and ill-constituted. He passed by my house 2 or 3 times a week to beg, was always poorly dressed and wore broken shoes. My family, and in particular my mother, taught me to treat Germán with respect and even affection. Amongst other injustices, he had to leave school because he needed to go to work to help his younger sisters, who just like him suffered from their condition.

One day, I was in the centre of my city and I suddenly felt unwell; I wanted to go home soon but did not have the money to take a taxi. At that very moment, Germán showed up with his broken shoes as usual and seeing my situation offered me his help. He gave me the equivalent of about $20 to go home by taxi and told me not to worry about it. I promised to return the money the next time we met.

Even to this day, the actions of Germán bewilder me, and I am still unable to understand how someone with all the shortcomings that he has had throughout his life is able to help others with such generosity. Unfortunately, Germán was born to a poor family and never managed to finish his studies. He has sadly spent some time in prison, and as a result of this he now has difficulty finding adequate employment. These circumstances mean that Germán will live in poverty and vulnerability in the same way his children are likely to follow. It's a great shame that people, as a result of the misfortune of being born under certain conditions are convicted in advance despite how good they may be intrinsically.

The lack of opportunities excludes people, breeds violence and insecurity, weakens cultural development and causes unhappiness. Enough evidence already exists to not see that the fight against inequality as antagonistic to economic growth. A developed economy is necessarily a just economy and offers equal opportunities. The pursuit of economic and social development should thus be based on the basis of equality of opportunity, a truly democratic and representative political system. These ideas stem from my life experience of knowing and living in countries where equity is understood as necessary and desirable. It also stems from having grown in an unequal country and highly tolerant of abuse showing a huge tolerance to the misfortune of people like Germán. Strangely, and unintending, my work focuses around the concept that a poor distribution of opportunities has a negative impact on development. It is thus very gratifying to see that the conclusions drawn from my life experience have finally found support in the findings of my doctoral dissertation.

During all this time spent writing my dissertation, I often felt that I could not progress and felt I was failing. In those moments, I thought many times of Germán and my parent's efforts to educate me and support my decision to come to Germany. Living in the beautiful city of Goettingen, flooded by young people of all nationalities is the perfect climate to develop ideas and learn about life. This city, which has hosted more than forty Nobel Prizes, has been the perfect place to write my dissertation and this would not have been possible had it not been for the support of many people I want to thank.

First I want to thank my parents Marcos Villalobos and Vicky Barría for the years of effort and support, my niece Camila Ignacia Villalobos Cisterna (a source of inspiration), my brothers Marcos and Rodrigo. Also to all those who, like Germán, had a word of encouragement when I felt alone or overwhelmed; to my friends of all nationalities; to those with whom I would talk about saving the planet. I would like to give my most sincere thanks to Leontina Steflic and Tessa Träger for their company, friendship and having always been there to help and listen.

I would also like to thank all those who are part of the Chair in Development Economics and Ibero-America Institute for Economic Research. In particular, I want to thank the director of both institutions who was also my professor, guide and mentor all this time, Prof. Dr. Stephan Klasen; thank you very much for having believed and trusted in me, and for giving me the opportunity to develop myself in a career I enjoy more and more. For giving me the freedom to develop my research and always being willing to listen and help me in everything I need. Thanks also for having facilitated my participation in more than fifteen international conferences that have shown me much of the world. Thanks professor, without you this would not have been possible.

I also thank the institutions that took care of me during long stays, such as the DIW-Berlin and UNU-WIDER in Helsinki. Thanks to all with whom I interacted in these institutions. Thank you for your hospitality and for giving me the opportunity to improve my skills as a researcher. I also thank Dr. Thomas Otter, for having invited me to collaborate with his research and for giving me friendship and advice.

I would like to dedicate this last paragraph to my parents whom I love. Thank you very much for joining me in my quest, for showing me that happiness is not in material things but in cultivating a life in love, friendship and understanding. I want to thank my mother for instilling in me a love for my neighbour and my father for being the man that I aspire to be like.

Although I've been far away for too long, I have always carried you with me in my heart. Without you, I would have never made it, thank you very much.

List of Tables

List of Figures

List of Abbreviations

CAFTA	Central America Free Trade Agreement
CASEN	Encuesta de Caracterización Socioeconómica Nacional, Chile
DGEEC	Dirección General de Estadísticas Encuestas y Censos, Paraguay
ECLAC	The Economic Commission for Latin America
EPH	Encuesta Permanente de Hogares, Paraguay
EPHPM	Encuesta Permanente de Hogares de Propósitos Múltiples, Honduras
HIPC	Heavily Indebted Poor Countries
IADB	Inter-American Development Bank
JICA	Japan International Cooperation Agency
MDRI	The Multilateral Debt Relief Initiative
MEC	Ministerio de Educación y Cultura, Paraguay
MIDEPLAN	Ministerio de Planificación, Chile
NELM	New Economics of Labour Migration
OECD	Organisation for Economic Co-operation and Development
PNUD	Programas de las Naciones Unidas para el Desarrollo
PRAF	Programa de Asignación Familiar, Honduras
RER	Real Exchange Rate
SENAEH	Honduran Secretary for Labour
SNEPE	Sistema Nacional de Evaluación del Proceso Educativo, Paraguay
STAR	Steps to Achieving Resilience Program
UN	United Nations
UNDP	United Nations Development Programme
UNESCO	United Nations Educational, Scientific and Cultural Organization
OREALC	Oficina Regional de Educación para América Latina y el Caribe
SPS	Survey of Primary Schools, Paraguay
WDI	World Development Indicators
WEI	World Education Indicators
WIDER	World Institute for Development Economics Research

Introduction and Overview

In many parts of the world, this century has brought about the most varied forms of expressions of discontent; all of which convey a desire for greater degrees of social justice, inclusion and equal opportunities. It seems, however, that all these ideas are not being properly represented within political systems. It is worth mentioning that these demonstrations are taking place in different countries with very different characteristics; from the U.S. to the Arab countries and from Spain to Chile. However, all these have something in common and that is the vision of a just and inclusive society based on the principle of equal opportunities under democracy. Few protesters claim today what Harry Frankfurt once called an “economic egalitarism”.[1] Citizens of developed countries demand "fair play", where the losses as well as the gains in welfare are distributed in a consistent manner. Meanwhile, citizens of developing countries claim for "an evening out" process by which the benefits of economic progress will serve to improve the welfare of everyone and thus progress will be achieved towards overcoming poverty and inequality.

As for overcoming poverty, the Millennium Development Goals (MDGs) reflect efforts to institutionalize the fight against poverty in eight goals, 18 targets and 48 technical indicators to measure progress towards its achievement. The MDGs recognize poverty as a multidimensional condition and whose implication is that the well-being should not be reduced to a problem of a lack of money, its measurement needing to be supplemented by direct indicators, such as for example status and access to health and education. Cornia et al. (2008) argues that the inclusion of nonmonetary indications amongst the MDGs reveals that such indicators measure structural dimensions of the human well-being. In spite of many countries having reduced their poverty levels over the past decades, people also demand greater levels of equity. Regarding the relevance of inequality, Wilkinson and Pickett (2010) studied the 23 richest countries in the world with populations greater than three million providing adequate data for comparison. They conclude that economic inequality is the main determinant of all social problems such as reduced life expectancy, mental illness, child mortality, violence and educational failure amongst other problems. Wider income gaps are harmful to the wellbeing of almost everyone in the society, not only the

1 Harry Frankfurt (1987) defines economic egalitarianism as “the doctrine that there should be no inequalities in the distribution of money”.

poor. The main implication of this is that solving these problems depends on the ability to reduce economic inequality.[2]

In general, it may be argued that the largest portion of those manifesting demanding equal opportunity would tolerate inequality as long as opportunity is widely available. However, how to achieve equal opportunities is a complex matter. Bell (1973) argues that equal opportunities require the elimination of birth, nepotism, patronage or any other criterion different than the "fair" competition open equally to talent and ambition to allocate the position that an individual holds in the educational system and in the labour market. Under a simplified framework, I believe that equal opportunities mean to be properly prepared for a social and productive life, having equal opportunities to access good-quality jobs and compensations regardless of birth, race, gender, or other characteristics that might be considered arbitrary or beyond an individual's control. In simple words, it means to provide a levelled playing field. In each of the essays, the problem of inequality is addressed from a different angle; however, the overall conclusion of this thesis, which focuses on studying the labour market in countries such as Paraguay, Honduras and Chile, shows that although certain individuals have adverse family backgrounds, this has permanent effects on their job performance. Adverse family backgrounds are associated with fewer employment opportunities, precarious employment or underemployment, the inability to migrate in search of better job opportunities and greater degrees of vulnerability when there are structural economic changes. Unfortunately, poor job performance of relatively large portions of the population results in low levels of income, poverty and vulnerability that are passed on to the next generation.

Essay 1 analyzes the dynamics of the income inequality change in the highly dualistic economy of Honduras between 1991 and 2007. This study was part of the UNU-WIDER project 'The New Policy Model, Inequality and Poverty in Latin America: Evidence from the Last Decade and Prospects for the Future' and it is the base of our contributing chapter to the textbook edited by Prof. Andrea Cornia "Falling Inequality in Latin America. Policy Changes and Lessons", published by the Oxford University Press.

Honduras stands out in Latin America as one of the few examples where inequality has not declined in the early 2000s, as in most other Latin American countries. Honduras has thus been an outlier where the peak in inequality occurred much later and the decline thereafter is also much more tentative. The macro and micro causes of this exceptionalism are the main topic of this paper.

---

2 Sen (1997) points out the importance in going from income inequality to economic inequality which is a much broader concept.

Honduras is a small open economy relying heavily on a narrow range of exports, mainly bananas and coffee, making it highly vulnerable to shifts in commodity prices and natural disasters. Hurricane Mitch largely wiped out the banana production in 1998 and 1999, from which Honduras recovered slowly thereafter. Additionally, the Honduran economy was damaged by falling coffee prices until about 2002 and benefited by rising prices for both commodities thereafter. However, investments in U.S. factories operated in Honduras under preferential tariff programs and non-traditional export sectors are slowly diversifying the production of the Honduran economy. Honduras is the fastest growing remittance destination in the region with inflows representing over a quarter of the GDP, equivalent to nearly three-quarters of all exports.

The country began to liberalize its international trade in 1990. As a result, total imports increased enormously. At the same time, the growth of Honduran exports lagged well behind the surge in imports. After the 1994 crisis, where the exchange rate was drastically depreciated, GDP growth resumed and the country witnessed improved public finances, a reduction of inflation and an increase of international reserves. Nevertheless, the trade imbalance continued to grow, real interest rates increased until 2002, and the real exchange rate continued to appreciate steadily until the same year. The appreciation of the real exchange rate seems to be linked to significant capital inflows received after Hurricane Mitch and donor transfers for reconstruction, and more recently by increased remittances, aid and debt relief.

But what are the channels of this disequalization of the income distribution? In order to answer this question, Essay 1, based on a methodology proposed by Barros et al. (2006), identifies and quantifies these inequality changes due to change in demographics, labour markets, remittances (international), government transfers (social policies) and other non-labour income (principally capital incomes and domestic private transfers). It relies on series of counterfactual simulations.

During the nineties, while in urban areas, the slight equalization of the household per-capita income distribution is driven by changes in non-labour income per adult, in rural areas, the story seems to be pretty much the same as what we observe at the country level, where the distribution of monthly earnings is the main disequalizing factor. Between 1999 and 2005, labour earnings are by far the more important inequality driver. Additionally, we find a limited impact of non-labour income on inequality changes. This impact is broken down into remittances, on the one hand, and other non-labour income on the other. At a country level and in rural areas, the impact is almost nonexistent, while in urban areas, the impact is slightly disequalizing. Finally, the period between 2005 and 2007 is characterized by a strong equalization in the household per-capita income distribution with a decrease of 5.2 Gini points at the country level, and of 7.3 and 3.2 Gini points in rural and urban areas, respectively. It is worth noting that changes in labour and non-labour income are responsible, almost in equal proportions, for the equalization pattern observed at the country level during this period. However, labour incomes appear to be more relevant in rural areas than in urban areas as a driver for reducing inequality. On the other hand, non-labour income are extraordinarily equalizing in all areas explaining about 43% of the equalization in rural areas and about 80% in urban areas.

Summarizing, changes in the distribution of labour incomes are by far the greatest contributor to the disequalization of the household per-capita income distribution between 1991 and 2005, particularly at the country level and in rural areas where most of the inequality change took place. In order to assess the relevance of the various factors on income inequality changes, handling whole distributions instead with averages, a micro-econometric decomposition methodology first proposed by Bourguignon et al. (1998) was tailored and applied to the Honduran case. Changes in unobservables (prices and endowments) and in the structure of education, together with a pronounced occupational sorting associated with an increasing productivity gap between the tradable and non-tradable sectors, represent the main drivers of the disequalization between 1991 and 2005. Regarding unobservable factors, it is plausible that the relative expansion of the non-agricultural sector during the 1990s, which demands a wider set of skills, is behind the extraordinary contribution of the unobservable to the increase in labour income inequality. Contrary to this, during the 2000s, the equalizing contribution of changes in the structure of formal education, together with a recovery of the tradable sector - driven by favourable external conditions and improved export revenues - promote equality by increasing labour earnings in the tradable sector, expressed as a reduction in the price to occupations (occupational sorting), and an equalizing impact of changes in unobservable factors on inequality.

Finally, Essay 1 presents an application of a methodology decomposition of a distributional change proposed by the author in Essay 2. Between 1991 and 1999, results show that the exogenous macroeconomic shift between the tradable and non-tradable sectors (occupation) explains a minimum of 8% of the observed disequalization at the country level. The contribution tends to be higher in the later periods contributing up to 40% of the disequalization between 1999 and 2005. After 2005, the commodity boom seems to have reversed the tradable-non-tradable shift, but whether it is able to overcome the other structural causes of rising inequality, is hard to predict at present. The presented methodology in Essay 2 aims to link findings from the micro-econometric decomposition by Bourguignon et al. (1998) with the macroeconomic story. The mentioned methodology assumes workers' heterogeneity (allowing correlation between mobility costs and skills) causing an insufficient mobility of workers between tradable and non-tradable sectors (inducing a positive sloped non-tradable labour supply) and skill capital complementarity. Therefore, different equilibrium labour earnings across sectors determine the observed wage gap between sectors. This formulation is compatible with the model by Devillanova et al. (2010) which also relies on the complementarity between the two types of labour. The prediction of this formulation is that an economy suffering a sectoral shift against the backward sector will increase the inequality between and within sectors.

We argue that the underlying determinant of the disequalization is the relatively low mobility between sectors and occupations of less-skilled workers, where typically a poor agricultural worker is unable to abandon his sector and change to other sectors or occupations. As shown Essay 2, improvements in productivity tend to cancel the wage-gap between the tradable and non-tradable sectors and also ensure higher labour income levels, while improvements in mobility between sectors lead to an accelerated decrease in this gap. We argue that the rising international competitiveness through policies promoting the productivity of the tradable sectors, at the expense of other sectors, increases the standard of living in the country, when compared with treating the other sectors equally.

Turning to Chile, although the dynamic growth experienced during the past two decades, there is a consensus that the improvement of the standards of living has not been equally distributed across regions or communes. In a context where it is expected that internal migration may work as a mechanism to equalize relative resource scarcities over regions, Soto and Torche (2004) show evidence that migration has become increasingly less important as an equalizing mechanism for regional disparities. Based on this evidence, Essay 3 focuses on the determinants of inter-communal movements of workers aiming to understand how the selection process of the migrant population is. It considers observed and unobserved characteristics, productivity differentials and initial conditions allowing to asses which factors are currently discouraging migration and thus hampering the equalization of living standards. The empirical approach of this paper consists of a switching regression model presented by Goldfeld and Quandt (1973) with endogenous switching (Maddala, 1983) which can be properly used as a counterpart from an extended Roy model in the migration context. The used methodology contributes through the provision of a structural form for internal migration, which is derived from a powerful theoretical framework.

Evidence has been found that the potential wage differential strongly determines the probability to move, but only when the differential reaches some determined threshold for individuals with mean characteristics (about 0.5 and 0.3 log-points for workers originating from rural and urban communes respectively). This evidence supports the idea that migration can be seen as an investment decision. However, the potential wage differential for most individuals is relatively small compared to the migration costs. This explains why migration is a rare phenomena being unable to reduce regional disparities. Moreover, migration not only depends on individual characteristics, but strongly relies on the household education. Unfortunately, this evidence indicates that it is highly possible that the one who is migrating is not necessarily the one who may benefit from higher labour incomes at the destination (observing high potential wage differentials and therefore, contributing to equalize outputs across regions), but the one who is not being constrained by its household. Contrary to this, the one who may probably take advantage from labour market differentials, but belongs to a household with low levels of education, will probably be forced to stay. Thus, household-level migration costs are a source of inefficiency when labour markets allocate workers between rural and urban communes. Finally, this study suggests that supporting the supply side in the rural economy is not the only way to achieve convergence across the territory. Subsidies aimed to reduce migration costs can also be considered under a framework oriented towards encouraging functional migration flows. Thus, this paper supports the main idea of the New Economics of Labour Migration Theory, considering migration as a household decision (Stark and Bloom, 1985 and Stark 1993).

Turning to education, the idea that schooling scores depend on a combination of family background characteristics, ability and school-institutional related variables is well-accepted. Regarding the issue of intergenerational transmission of inequality in the educational system, the degree to which a better institutional performance of the school service can compensate problems originated in the family background is crucial. In the case of Paraguay, despite the significant progress achieved in recent years regarding access to education and school permanence, the country still faces great challenges. These include the problems of internal efficiency, quality in learning and equity. Essay 4 merges three different data sets and uses the mathematics and communication scores in its pure form (non-logarithmic) as dependent variables. In general, the way our model is specified, it can be understood as a reduced form specification where the coefficients change in their scope according to the specification of the education production function.

By providing integral health solutions, minimizing under-nutrition and providing good conditions in the classroom, training teachers (according to their gaps) can impact positively on low and mean learning outcomes, thus contributing to an improved educational quality and breaking cycles of intergenerational transmission of inequality. Moreover, the equality approach should focus on trying to improve the worst scores and our results show that this can be reached at a significant level closing teacher training gaps, improving classroom conditions and improving health and nutrition. To ask education policies to focus their efforts regarding inequality-reducing measures on lower income quintiles should not be that difficult, given that an important part of students from higher income quantiles are enrolled in private education. Unfortunately, any action taken by public policies to reduce inequality will have, in the short run, a limited impact regarding its possibility to reduce the intergenerational transmission of (welfare) inequality, since family background is a much stronger force in determining the persistence of high inequality levels.

Essay 1 - The dynamics of inequality change in a highly dualistic economy: Honduras, 1991-2007[i]

Abstract

We examine the drivers of inequality change in Honduras between 1991 and 2007, trying to understand why inequality increased in Honduras until 2005, while it was falling in most other Latin American countries. Using annual household surveys, we document first rising inequality between 1991and 2005, which is followed by falling inequality thereafter. Using an inequality decomposition technique, we show that the rising inequality between 1991 and 2005 was, for the most part, driven by the dispersion of labour incomes in rural areas. We also show that the extraordinary labour earnings disequalization is mainly the result of a widening wage gap between the tradable and non-tradable sectors and occupations, combined with highly segmented labour markets and poor overall educational progress. The underlying determinants of the divergence between tradable and non-tradable sectors were highly overvalued currencies and poor commodity process for Honduras' agricultural exports. Between 2005 and 2007, however, the inequality reduction was a result of equalizing trends in labour and non-labour income. The commodity boom promoting the tradable sector and remittances (in this order) played a significant role here, with government transfers playing a small supporting role. Since the decline in inequality is largely driven by international factors, we cannot be sure whether the decline in inequality will continue.

---

[i] Based on a joint work with Stephan Klasen and Thomas Otter. This study is the base of our chapter contributing to the textbook edited by Prof. Andrea Cornia "Falling Inequality in Latin America. Policy Changes and Lessons", published by Oxford University Press.

1.1 Introduction

Honduras stands out in Latin America as one of the few examples where inequality has not declined in the early 2000s, as in most other Latin American countries. As we show below, inequality has been rising, more or less continuously between 1991 and 2005. After 2005, inequality has started to fall, apparently extending beyond the last data point in our analysis, 2007.[3] Honduras has thus been an outlier where the peak in inequality occurred much later and the decline thereafter is also much more tentative. The macro and micro causes of this exceptionalism are the main topic of this paper.

Despite considerable economic growth before the global economic downturn started in 2008, the World Bank (2006a) portrays Honduras as one of the poorest countries in Latin America with more than 50% of its population below the poverty line. Moreover, the country has one of the highest rates of inequality in Latin America. Poverty and inequality, in particular, have been aggravated by natural disasters (such as Hurricane Mitch in 1998)[4] since the poor commonly live off small-scale agriculture in rural areas.[5] After the disaster of Hurricane Mitch, Honduras designed a Poverty Reduction Strategy, seeking to reduce extreme poverty by half by 2015 (World Bank, 2006b), and its implementation since 2006 has been supported by debt relief from donors through the HIPC Initiative. These actions, together with external market conditions, have allowed Honduras to experience a positive economic growth during the last 15 years, averaging 3% annually.

Honduras is a small open economy relying heavily on a narrow range of exports, mainly bananas and coffee, making it highly vulnerable to natural disasters and shifts in commodity prices. In particular, Hurricane Mitch largely wiped out the banana production in 1998 and 1999, from which Honduras recovered very slowly thereafter, and was greatly affected by falling coffee prices until about 2002 and rising prices for both commodities thereafter (see Figure A.1 in

3 2007 is the most recent year for which reliable household survey data are available (Encuesta Permanente de Hogares: EPHPM I from 1991-99 and II from 2001-07.) We always use the October wave of the survey. Since 2008, only the May wave has been available. These show that the decline in inequality has apparently continued beyond 2007 (EPHPM 2008, 2009 and 2010).

4 ECLAC (1999) states "Hurricane Mitch is the most serious hydro-meteorological disaster to have struck Central America in many years. Its force upon reaching the coasts of the region was exceptional, as were its diameter, the amount of moisture and rain it carried and the erratic path it followed for several days". Moreover, Mitch caused around 14,000 direct deaths and an estimated material loss of around US$3.8 billion.

5 EPHPM 2007 shows that 85% and 64% of individuals of the first and second quintiles, respectively, are living in rural areas.

the Appendix). However, investments in the "*maquila*" (U.S. factories operated in Honduras under preferential tariff programs) and non-traditional export sectors are slowly diversifying the production of the Honduran economy. These attempts at diversification are supported by signing and ratifying the U.S.-Central America Free Trade Agreement (CAFTA). Honduras is also notable for its very high population growth rate of more than 2 % yearly throughout the period under examination. With such a rapidly growing labour force, it also exports its labour and is in fact the fastest growing remittance destination in the region with inflows representing over a quarter of the GDP, equivalent to nearly three-quarters of all exports. Consequently, external conditions, trade and currency policy will have an important impact on growth, poverty, and inequality.

Honduras has recurrently faced serious economic crisis; in 1994, 1998/9 and then again in 2009. These crises were often disequalizing, because of the lack of available proper safety nets for poor and vulnerable population groups (Lustig, 1995). Despite improvements in tax collections and other macro-economic policies, the country continues to struggle with fiscal deficits.[6] Since 2005, as a result of the combined effects of public policies (targeted social transfers),[7] improved economic growth closely linked to increasing commodity prices and the fact that significant additional resources have gone directly to households through remittances,[8] there has been a reduction in extreme poverty.

The political system in Honduras of the past 30 years has been characterized by the Liberal Party (social liberal political party) and the National Party (centre-right conservative political party) taking turns in government. As a result, there is not much variation in the kinds of policies implemented. Tax revenues have been growing continuously since 1994, beginning with Carlos Reina's government. The same occurs with the public social expenditure. It may be argued, that liberal governments have been slightly more willing to increasing debt-based social expenditure, while governments led by the National Party have been more conservative in this policy aspect. Regarding labour market policies, even when there are some labour regulations protecting workers, these regulations are quite flexible and have been systematically ignored by the government and by companies. As a result, there is much evidence on job insecurity, which remains almost unchanged. The last liberal government of Zelaya (since 2006) took a more populist turn, expanding social programmes and minimum wages,

6 See Cardemil et al. (2000).

7 US$ 71.5 million accumulated between 2005 and 2007 according to the Honduran Secretary of Finance.

8 In 2008, remittances reached US$ 2.8 billion corresponding to 18% of GDP (Central Bank of Honduras, 2010).

and was subsequently ousted in 2009 by the military. After renewed presidential elections Lobo from the National Party was installed in 2010.

1.1.1 Macroeconomic environment, liberalization and trade imbalance

Honduras began to liberalize its international trade in 1990.[9] As a result, total imports increased enormously; almost 12% per annum during 1990-1995, and afterwards even faster. At the same time, the growth of Honduran exports lagged well behind the surge in imports (see Figure 1.1). After the 1994 crisis where the exchange rate was drastically depreciated, GDP growth resumed and the country witnessed improved public finances, a reduction of inflation and an increase of international reserves (see Table 1.1).[10] Nevertheless, the trade imbalance continued to grow, real interest rates increased until 2002, and the real exchange rate continued to appreciate steadily until the same year (see Table A.4 in the Appendix).[11] The appreciation of the real exchange rate (RER) seems to be linked to significant capital inflows received after Hurricane Mitch and donor transfers for reconstruction, and more recently by increased remittances, aid and debt relief. Paz Cafferata (2003) argues that this happened despite sterilization policies of the Central Bank which proved to be insufficient.

The Honduran growth has been accompanied by low investment rates inducing a weak modernization in the productive sectors. These conditions did not facilitate an improved productivity. According to Lugones et al. (2007), the annualized change rate of the total factor productivity was -1.24 per cent between 1991 and 2003.[12] Figure 1.1 shows how GDP growth is closely correlated with the expansion in the total amount of working hours during the 1990s.[13] In contrast, the 2000s are characterized by higher rates of gross fixed capital formation and declining real interest rates (starting in 2002) and a divergence between the rates of expansion of labour and real GDP.

---

9 Through the Macroeconomic Policy Reform Law in March 1990.

10 Total GDP grew at an annual average rate of 4.5% between 1994 and 1997, after which this trend was interrupted by Hurricane Mitch. International reserves increased from US$205 million to US$1,248 million. The fiscal deficit, excluding international transfers, dropped almost five percentage points from 8% to 3% of the GDP during the period between 1994 and 2000.

11 See also Paz Cafferata (2003).

12 Total factor productivity is commonly understood, though not without controversy, as a proxy of technological change.

13 This employment index equals the unity in 2005 and represents 102.3 million working hours per week.

Table 1.1: Relevant macroeconomic indicators for selected periods (averages)

Indicator	1991-99	1999-2005	2005-07
Remittances/GDP* (since 2000)	n/a	10.8	20.1
Exports of goods and services/GDP*	40.6	52.9	56.1
Imports of goods and services/GDP*	47.7	67.8	78.6
Banana price index (until 2009)	86.4	123.2	196.4
Coffee price index (until 2009)	112.2	90.3	154.7
Current account balance/GDP*	-6.5	-5.6	-5.3
Average inflation rate	18.9	10.7	6.4
Maximal inflation rate	28.8	30.8	7.2
Real exchange rate (2000=100)	121.8	99.8	99.0
Real interest rate	19.36	9.26	7.10
Overall balance central government/GDP*	-3.2	-3.48	-2.13
Debt/GDP*	120.8	69.1	32.6
Tax revenues/GDP*	13.2	14.1	15.4
Public social spending/GDP*	5.92	8.92	9.90
Public social security spending/GDP*	0.28	0.22	0.36

Note: * percentages.

Source: Based on WDI, Secretaría Ejecutiva Consejo Monetario Centroamericano, Central Bank of Honduras (2010), ECLAC (1999).

This divergence may be the consequence of productivity improvements.[14] However, these averages do not let us see just how unequal the improvement (deterioration) of the labour productivity has been across the working population which we discuss below.

As in many developing countries (and in contrast to the richer middle-income economies of Latin America), the agricultural sector employs more people than any other sector. Although other sectors have been gaining importance, the agricultural sector still provides over one-third of jobs overall and over 55% in rural areas. Improvements in the agrarian production have not translated into higher labour incomes, presumably because of stagnant productivity given the low competitiveness of this sector, partly a consequence of the appreciated RER, insufficient capital investment, and the effects of the Hurricane Mitch on infrastructure and soil productivity.[15] After 2005, the commodity price booms in cof-

14 It is possible to observe in Figure 1.1 that the slope of the employment expansion is not decreasing over time.

15 For instance, between 1991 and 1999, the number of tractors per 100 km^2 increased by about 13%, while the number of workers in the agricultural sector rose by 19% during

fee and bananas significantly improved the situation in the agricultural tradable sector, a development that has continued to this day.[16]

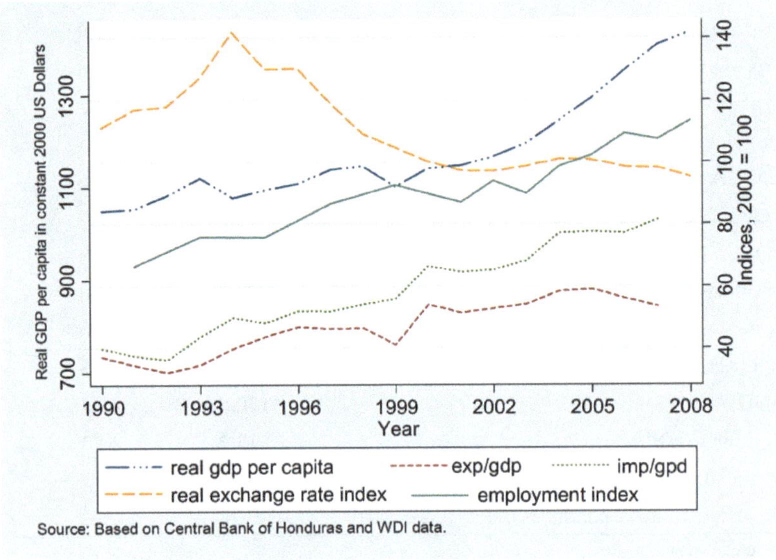

Figure 1.1: Selected macroeconomic indicators, 1990-2008

Contrary to this, and consistent with the appreciation of the RER since the early 1990s, the non-tradable sector appears to gain momentum. During the last two decades, a shift in the productive path, value generation and labour earnings can be observed. Household surveys show that earnings in agriculture, as a share of total earnings, declined from 28% in 1991 to 20% in 1999 and to 17% in 2007, while the share of labour incomes in non-tradable sectors such as commerce, transport, construction and basic services grew from 29% in 1991 to 39% in 2007. Other tradable sectors such as the manufacturing sector (*maquiladoras*) maintain a constant employment share.[17]

the same period. From 1991 to 2007, both figures have grown by about 40%, also driven by rapid population growth. These facts may support the idea that the productivity of labour, at least within agricultural activities, has been decreasing during the 1990s in part because of a reduction of units of capital per worker.

16 See Figure A.1 in the Appendix for a development of coffee and banana prices.

17 Figures obtained based on EPHPM I and II.

1.1.2 Sector-related changes in earnings: tradables versus non-tradables

An overvaluation of the RER will induce a loss of relative competitiveness of the tradable sector while favouring the non-tradable sector. The tradable sector consists of formal and informal employment of agriculture and livestock activities, mining and manufacture. The non-tradable sector consists of formal and informal employment in basic services (electricity, water, and gas), construction, commerce, transport, financing and other services. This hypothesis is supported in Figure 1.2, which shows that in both rural and urban areas, there is a rising gap between labour earnings in the non-tradable and the tradable sectors. Remarkably, this is true even if considering the fact that a considerable share of non-tradable employment are informal sector activities with low earnings. In fact, it turns out that in the early 1990s, earnings at the low end of the earnings distribution of the non-tradable sector were below those at the low end in the tradable sector. By 2005, the earnings in the non-tradable sector were considerably above those in the tradable sector. Consequently, the tradable sector has relatively declined over the last two decades.[18]

How would the expansion of the non-tradable sector affect inequality? The answer depends on the initial levels of inequality within and between the two sectors, and on how efficient labour markets are in reallocating workers from the tradable to the non-tradable sector. If workers can be reallocated easily, we would not expect large effects as workers move across sectors with little loss of earnings. Figure 1.3 shows evidence of this issue in rural areas. While low-earners in the tradable sector (top panels) suffered steep real earnings declines between 1991 and 2005, low-earners in the non-tradable sector seem to have kept their labour income stable between 1991 and 1999, and even improved their performance between 1999 and 2005. Why were low earners in the tradable sector not able to move to the non-tradable sector and profit from growing labour incomes?

18 According to household surveys, the share of wages in the tradable sector in rural areas declined from 67% of total wages in 1991 to 56% in 2007 (and from 25% and 22% of wages in urban areas).

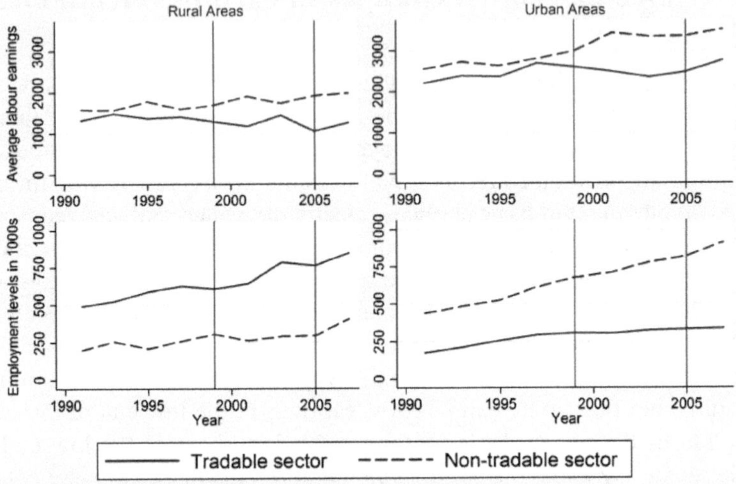

Note: Avg. labour earnings in Lempiras of 1999.
Source: Authors' calculations based on EPHPM I and EPHPM II.

Figure 1.2: Earnings and employment: tradable and non-tradable sectors, 1991-2007

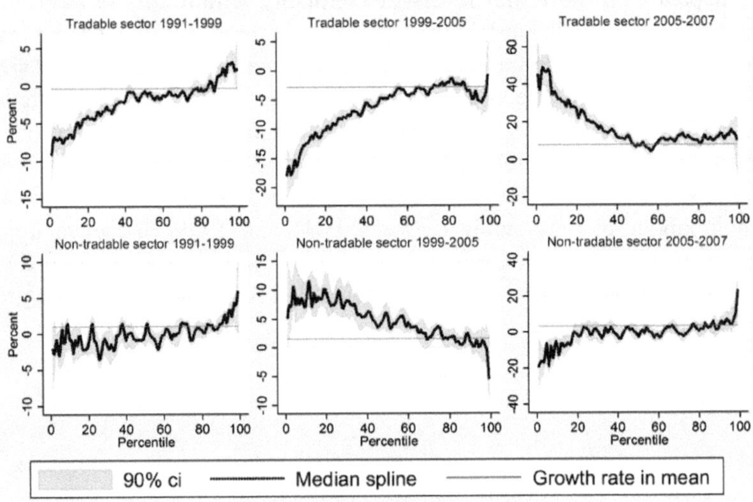

Note different y-axis scales.
Source: Authors' calculations based on EPHPM I and EPHPM II

Figure 1.3: Growth incidence curves: monthly earnings in the tradable and non-tradable sectors in rural areas, 1991-2007

The hypothesis here is that, in an economy where mobility cost changes across skill levels (observables and unobservables) with a technology exhibiting capital-skill complementarity, neo-liberal policies allowing a decline in the tradable sector will translate into the (considerable) disequalization of labour incomes during this period (1991-2005).

Given that the free-trade openness is the more relevant structural change taking place during the 1990s in Honduras, the next section covers the relationship between international trade and inequality. Moreover, the main conclusions of a model by Devillanova et al. (2010) explaining the consequences of a trade-induced sectoral shift on inequality will be presented. The model is based on workers' heterogeneity and capital-skill complementarity, which appear to be realistic assumptions for the Honduran economy.

1.1.3 Workers' heterogeneity and capital-skill complementarity

There is much evidence which suggests that income inequality increases after trade liberalization takes place. López-Calva and Lustig (2010) state that many Latin American governments adopted market-oriented reforms to pull the economy out of crisis. They argue that the inequality increase during the 1990s was partially driven by a significant increase in relative returns to tertiary education and that this was consistent with a skill-biased technological change after the adoption of trade liberalization reforms.[19]

According to the predictions of the classical trade models, the 1995-2002 RER overvaluation and declining commodity prices possibly encouraged a reallocation of factors towards the non-tradable sector in Honduras. Given this, there is evidence that the imperfect mobility of workers would translate into low levels of labour reallocation reducing the benefits of trade integration (see Papageorgiou et al., 1991 and Wacziarg and Wallack, 2004). Additionally, according to Devillanova et al. (2010), if moving costs and skills are correlated and there is capital-skill complementarity, a trade-induced sectoral shift would increase

[19] See Gasparini and Cruces (2010), Cragg and Eppelbaum (1996) and Jaramillo and Saavedra (2010). Figure 1.6 shows that this is true for Honduras between 1990 and 1995, at least in rural areas. This is a period characterized by a strong devaluation and the opening up of the economy. Note that the rise in the skill premium can be explained by an increasing demand for those with secondary-level education or higher in rural areas. Thereafter, the Honduran economy faces a continuous appreciation of the RER and declining commodity prices until 2002.

wage inequality between different skill levels in a sector and within skill levels across sectors (Figures 2 and 5 in Devillanova et al., 2010).

The assumption of a positive correlation between skills and moving costs is based on the idea that highly educated workers develop more general abilities, which have a productive value across all sectors and occupations. Contrary to this, less-skilled workers are characterized by abilities that are typically less transferable. Devillanova et al. (2010) mention a variety of studies supporting the hypothesis of higher internal mobility of the more educated workers.[20] In Honduras, we additionally find that migrants are also more likely to belong to the more educated households.[21] Thus, the deplorable levels of education in rural areas will reinforce internal immobility, particularly for those in the tradable sector.[22]

Between 1991 and 1995, the opening up of trade and investment and the devaluation of the RER favoured the tradable sector. Here, the capital-skill complementarity might explain the one-time disequalizing effect of skill-biased technical change. A confirmation of this can be found in Figure 1.2, where until 1993, the wage gap between sectors seems to disappear.[23] Starting in 1994, the tradable sector faces important difficulties due to increasing real interest rates, the progressive appreciation of the RER together with declining commodity prices and Hurricane Mitch in 1998. On the other hand, the non-tradable sector shows increasing earnings, due to disproportionate investments as a result of the favourable macro-conditions (capital inflows). Consequently, this sector increases its skill intensity and skill premium. At the same time, relative labour incomes for unskilled workers also increase in the non-tradable sector (relative to those in the tradable sector). This occurs due to the complementarity between

20 The more educated workers find jobs easily and have lower transaction costs (Greenwood, 1975; Bednarzik, 1993 and Helwing, 2001). They also learn faster and are able to implement modern technologies and perform new activities more efficiently (Nelson and Phelps, 1966; Bartel and Lichtenberg, 1987). Moreover, they are more likely to change a job voluntarily (Magnani, 2001; Tomkins and Twomey, 2000). Here, internal mobility refers to movements across industry, sectors and geographical areas.

21 In section 1.5, we show the predicted migration flows accounting for productivity differentials. They are based on a structural probability model, which account for the self-selection bias in the rural-urban migration process. Results suggest that the household education is an important determinant of the migration probability. Villalobos Barría (2012) reaches the same conclusion for the rural-urban migration pattern in Chile during the period 2002-2006.

22 According to EPHPM 1999, rural workers belong to households with an average of 2.32 and 3.11 years of education in the tradable and non-tradable sectors, respectively.

23 Here, the wage disequalization is explained mainly through increasing returns to education (and skills).

the two types of labour and the insufficient migration of less-skilled workers towards the dynamic sector. Consequently, skilled and unskilled workers now perform better-off in the attractive sector (relative to those in the tradable sector), as shown in Figure 1.3. The labour income distribution becomes more unequal due to the evolution of the inter-sectoral wage gap taking place across the whole ability distribution.

Section 1.4 proposes a methodology to account for this evolution. It assesses the inequality effects of the observed change in the wage gap between sectors and aims to isolate the inequality changes related to the distribution of skills from those which are exclusively related to changes in the relative competitiveness of the tradable sector.

1.1.4 A dysfunctional and highly dualistic educational system

Average education in the Honduran labour force has increased only marginally over time (see Table 1.2). At the country level, during the period 1991-2007, the number of years of education of the Honduran labour force rose from only 5.1 to a still very poor 6.0. Furthermore, education lagged behind in rural areas; in 1991, urban labour force participants had over seven years of education (at about a secondary education level) versus 3.6 years of education in rural areas (less than a primary education level). Second, there are also marked differences regarding changes in the structure of educational levels, most likely linked to different educational opportunities as well as rural-urban migration (see below). Although the proportion without formal education has been steadily declining in urban and rural areas alike, in rural areas this was made up with increasing shares of people with intermediate education, while in urban areas the largest increase was among those with tertiary education.

The accelerated expansion of tertiary education in urban areas dominates changes in the distribution of education at the country level. Given the (often convex) link between education and earnings, educational progress in urban areas may serve to disperse the labour income distribution.[24]

24 The disequalization of the earnings distribution may occur even when the Gini coefficient of years of schooling shows a monotonic decreasing trend (1991-2007), which has been termed the 'paradox of progress.' In previous studies for Argentina and Mexico, the Gini for educational attainment declined while earnings inequality increased; see Gasparini et al. (2005) for Argentina and Legovini at al. (2005) for Mexico.

Table 1.2: Changes in the educational structure of the Honduran labour force, 1991-2007

	Per cent				Annualized change*		
Educational structure	1991	1999	2005	2007	1991-99	1999-2005	2005-07
Country level							
Without	20.0	16.7	14.3	13.2	-0.41	-0.41	-0.57
Less than secondary	57.8	58.0	57.0	56.0	0.02	-0.16	-0.54
Less than tertiary	18.1	20.0	21.9	23.1	0.23	0.33	0.56
Tertiary	4.1	5.3	6.7	7.8	0.16	0.24	0.54
Years of schooling	5.1	5.4	5.8	6.0	0.04	0.06	0.11
Gini coefficient	45.4	43.0	41.3	40.3	-0.30	-0.20	-0.10
Rural areas							
Without	27.4	24.1	21.2	19.3	-0.42	-0.48	-0.92
Less than secondary	64.3	65.5	67.7	67.0	0.14	0.37	-0.35
Less than tertiary	7.8	9.6	10.3	12.2	0.23	0.12	0.96
Tertiary	0.5	0.9	0.9	1.5	0.05	0.00	0.31
Years of schooling	3.6	3.8	3.9	4.2	0.03	0.02	0.15
Gini coefficient	47.6	45.8	43.6	42.4	-0.20	-0.30	-0.20
Urban areas							
Without	10.6	8.7	7.0	6.4	-0.23	-0.30	-0.30
Less than secondary	49.3	49.8	45.6	43.8	0.05	-0.69	-0.94
Less than tertiary	31.4	31.3	34.4	35.1	-0.01	0.51	0.33
Tertiary	8.7	10.2	13.0	14.8	0.19	0.47	0.91
Years of schooling	7.1	7.2	7.8	8.0	0.01	0.10	0.10
Gini coefficient	37.2	35.4	33.1	32.4	-0.20	-0.30	-0.10

Note: * in percentage points; Gini coefficient based on the years of schooling distribution.
Source: Authors' calculations based on data from EPHPM I and EPHPM II.

1.1.5 Education reforms and crisis during the 1990s

During the early 1990s, market-oriented reforms designed to pull economies out of a crisis were implemented in Honduras, including changes that affected educational policies. Barahona and Blas (2008) argue that reforms were implemented with the purpose of decentralizing and incorporating the private sector in the educational process.[25] Despite these efforts, the Honduran educational system is still deficient in coverage and quality.[26] Lack of funds, a shortage of

25 Private education has flourished during the last decades. Private schools do not have as much academic prestige in Honduras. Nevertheless, wealthy families choose to send their children to private schools because they still convey a higher social status and more amenities.

26 Following Barahona and Blas (2008), coverage was one of the central goals of the reform implemented by the government of Carlos Reina. However, decentralization and fragmentation of the administrative structure ended up with a reduced investment in ed-

teachers (particularly in rural areas), poor pedagogic training, and obsolete curricula are some problems which the Honduran educational system has to deal with.[27] Such problems are not surprising given the modest spending levels in education. Public spending in education in Honduras is far from the more advanced educational systems in Latin America. While public spending in education per-capita in Honduras reached US$40 in 2000, Argentina and Chile were spending US$520 and US$208 respectively.[28] However, just within the last decade, public spending in education in 2008 has doubled in absolute terms, reducing the gap to other countries. Unfortunately, given that public spending on education in Honduras is already quite high as a share of the GDP, considerable complementary financial flows will be required to enhance educational resources further.

1.1.6 Rural-urban migration

Changes in the structure of education of the labour force are a consequence of fertility rates, efficiency and coverage of the schooling system and migration. While fertility rates and the nature of the schooling system tend to change slowly over time, internal migration may have an extraordinary impact on origin and destination areas (rural and urban areas). In order to understand the contribution of internal migration on changes in the educational distribution and thus on inequality, we estimate migration flows in the origin controlling for the fact that, after migration, migrants in urban areas may decide to enrol or to continue current studies, and consequently, ex-post estimates of the structure of education overstate the educational attainment of rural-urban migrants at the time of migration.

For this reason, we estimated a structural model for internal migration based on the extended Roy model.[29] Table 1.3 compares the educational structure of the net migrant group with the observed structure in rural and urban areas in 1994 and 1999. By comparing both structures, it is clear that rural-urban migra-

ucation during the 1990s. As a result of this, even to this day, coverage deficiencies are particularly notorious in preschool and secondary levels and in rural areas.

27 Additionally, according to the background notes by the U.S. Department of State, Hurricane Mitch damaged more than 3,000 schools nationwide.

28 According to the ECLAC, Social Development Division.

29 The extended Roy model finds a suitable counterpart in a switching regression model, presented by Goldfeld and Quandt (1973) with endogenous switching (Maddala and Nelson, 1975; Maddala, 1983). Technical details about the estimation procedure are available upon request.

tion increases educational inequality in urban areas, as the share of migrants with no education by far exceeds the share of urban residents with no education.

Table 1.3: Structures of education for the net migrants and by areas, Honduras, 1994-1999

	Urban areas		Rural areas		Internal migrants	
	1994	1999	1994	1999	Net migrants	Structure
Without	9.34	8.88	22.49	22.07	43,799	23.74
Less than secondary	52.40	50.88	67.39	67.03	110,056	59.65
Less than tertiary	32.05	32.44	9.76	10.36	30,519	16.54
Tertiary	6.21	7.80	0.36	0.54	135	0.07

Note: The educational structure of migrants controls for the fact that some migration has taken place for education. See Villalobos Barría (2012) for further details.

Source: Authors' calculations based on EPHPM I and EPHPM II.

In contrast, it should reduce inequality in rural areas as migrants are disproportionately drawn from the high end (less than secondary) of the distribution of education. This must be kept in mind when interpreting changes in inequality. Finally, this result points out the validity of the workers' heterogeneity assumption (correlation between mobility costs and skills).[30]

1.1.7 Inequality change in Honduras

Figure 1.4 depicts inequality trends in household per-capita income and labour earnings. Inequality in household per-capita income increased steadily since 1991 over a period of more than ten years and started to decrease after 2005, a trend which appears to have continued beyond 2007, the last comparable data set in our analysis. The inequality increase appears to be heavily influenced by an increase of rural inequality (and possibly rural-urban shifts), while urban inequality changed very little during that time period. Moreover, changes in inequality at the country level appear to be closely related to increasing labour earnings inequality,[31] which also reaches its peak in 2005.[32]

30 This is because migration from rural to urban areas is, to some degree, overlapped with the migration from tradable (mainly agriculture) to the non-tradable sector.

31 See Figure A.2 in the Appendix.

32 The inequality peak is not driven by outliers. In order to check the robustness of our Gini estimates, we excluded the top and bottom 5% of observations from the income distributions. Trends are not affected by outliers and confirm the finding that in 2005 income inequality reached its highest level within the period of observation.

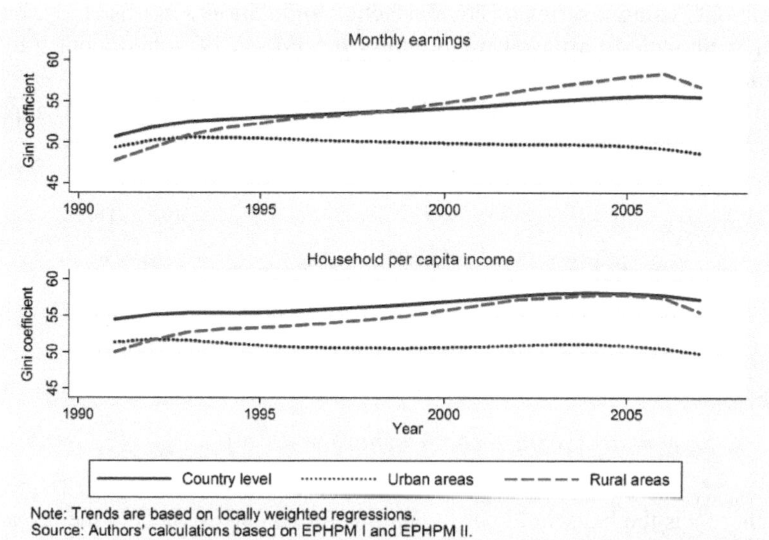

Figure 1.4: Monthly earnings and household per-capita income inequality trends, 1991-2007

Based on the discussion above, our hypothesis about inequality trends is that extremely low levels of human capital accumulation, particularly in rural areas, together with neo-liberal labour market institutions and an appreciated real exchange rate worsened rural incomes, in particular, those at the bottom of the distribution of the tradable sector. To analyze inequality change using various decomposition techniques, we divide our analysis into three periods, 1991-1999 (just after Hurricane Mitch), 1999-2005 (the year of highest inequality) and 2005-2007.

1.2 Micro-econometric decomposition I: The proximate determinants of changes in income inequality

In this section, we present evidence regarding the relative importance of demographics, labour markets, (international) remittances, government transfers (social policies) and other non-labour income (principally capital incomes and domestic private transfers) in explaining inequality changes in the distribution of household per-capita income between 1991 and 2007. Following the methodology proposed by Barros et al. (2006), we are able to identify and quantify these determinants using a series of counterfactual simulations. In this study, our extended methodology allowed us to assess the impact of government transfers, remittances and other non-labour income on inequality changes.

Putting technical aspects of the decomposition aside, the empirical approach is based on the following tree of identities:

$$y = a * r \tag{1}$$

$$r = o + t \tag{2}$$

$$t = u * w \tag{3}$$

$$o = rem + soc + nrs \tag{4}$$

Hence,

$$y = a * [(rem + soc + other) + u * w] \tag{5}$$

Where y is the household per-capita income, a corresponds to the proportion of working adults in the household, r the household income per adult, o corresponds to the household non-labour income per adult and t represents the household labour income per adult. The variable u represents the proportion of working adults in the household and w is the labour income per working adult in the household. Finally, in this extended specification (Identity (5)) remittances per adult in the household are symbolized by *rem*, while government transfers per adult in the household are represented by *soc*, and *other* represents other household non-labour income per adult. As mentioned by Barros et al. (2006), since we are dealing with identities, any change in the income distribution must be related to changes in the joint distribution of these proximate determinants.

To clarify our notation in Table 1.4, in the decomposition presented by Identity (1), for example, we defineΔ_a as the proportion of change of the Gini coefficient, resulting from changes in the distribution of the percentage of adults in the household.[33] In the same way Δ_r is the proportion of change of the Gini coefficient, resulting from changes in the distribution of the household income per adult. Finally, $\Delta_{a \to r}$ captures the proportion of change of the Gini coefficient resulting from changes in the association between the proportion of adults in household a and the household income per adult r. Using the same notation, the contribution caused by changes in the remaining proximate determinants, and their respective associations on changes in labour income inequality, are illus-

33 Since we estimate whole distributions, we strictly decompose distributional changes (which are evaluated using the Gini coefficient), rather than a direct change in the Gini coefficient.

trated in Table 1.4 (Identity (5)). Tables A.5 and A.6 in the Appendix show separate results for urban and rural areas.

Table 1.4: Percentage contribution of the proximate determinants to inequality changes of the household per-capital income, 1991-2007

	ΔGini = 2.7 points 1991-99			ΔGini = 4.2 points 1999-2005				ΔGini = -5.2 points 2005-07				
Determinant	(1)	(2)	(3)	(1)	(2)	(3)	(4)	(1)	(2)	(3)	(4)	(5)
$\Delta_{a\to r}$	-10.77	-10.77	-10.77	11.49	11.49	11.49	11.49	1.87	1.87	1.87	1.87	1.87
Δ_a	0.04	0.04	0.04	-3.16	-3.16	-3.16	-3.16	-2.93	-2.93	-2.93	-2.93	-2.93
Δ_r	110.7			91.7				-98.9				
$\Delta_{o\to t}$		11.10	11.10		-0.54	-0.54	-0.54		-2.72	-2.72	-2.72	-2.72
Δ_o		-24.23	-24.23		0.80	0.80			-51.2	-51.2		
Δ_t		123.86			91.41				-45.1			
$\Delta_{u\to w}$			-47.86			3.61	3.61			19.1	19.1	19.1
Δ_u			-2.18			10.29	10.29			-6.9	-6.9	-6.9
Δ_w			173.89			77.51	77.51			-57.3	-57.3	-57.3
$\Delta_{rem\to nrem}$							5.10				18.78	18.78
Δ_{rem}							-7.32				-43.6	-43.6
Δ_{nrem}							3.02				-26.3	
$\Delta_{soc\to other}$												10.22
Δ_{soc}												-11.74
Δ_{other}												-24.79
ΔTotal	100	100	100	100	100	100	100	-100	-100	-100	-100	-100

Note: Δ_r is decomposed in $\Delta_{o\to t} + \Delta_o + \Delta_t$ as Δ_t in $\Delta_{u\to w} + \Delta_u + \Delta_w$, Δ_o in $\Delta_{rem\to nrem} + \Delta_{rem} + \Delta_{nrem}$ and Δ_{nrem} in $\Delta_{soc\to nsoc} + \Delta_{soc} + \Delta_{nsoc}$.

Source: Authors' calculations based on EPHPM I and EPHPM II.

1.2.1 First sub-period: The nineties (1991-1999) – labour market-driven inequality increase

During this period, demographic changes a and their association with the distribution of the household income per adult $\Delta_{a\to r}$ contributed towards equalizing the per-capita household income distribution y, while the distribution of the household incomes per adult r explains about 110% of the disequalizing trend during this decade. By decomposing r, it is possible to assess the role of the household labour and non-labour income per adult, t and o respectively. While non-labour income were equalizing, labour incomes are the main driver in the observed inequality increase. When looking at household labour incomes per adult t, the decomposition presented in column (3) allows us to assess the role of changes in the proportion of working adults u and the importance of changes in monthly earnings per working adult w. While u is not capable of explaining any inequality change, changes in monthly earnings are by far the greatest contributor to the disequalization of y. The association between the distribution of employment and earnings reduces, to some extent, this extraordinary disequalizing force.

While in urban areas, the slight equalization of the household per-capita income distribution is driven by changes in non-labour income per adult, in rural areas the story seems to be pretty much the same as what we observe at the country level, where the distribution of monthly earnings is the main disequalizing factor.

1.2.2 Second sub-period: The nineties II (1999-2005) – labour market-driven inequality increase

This second period shows similar results as the decade of the 1990s; monthly earnings are by far the main inequality driver. The only notable difference is that in urban areas the distribution of employment explains almost one-fourth of the 2.4 Gini points increase between 1999 and 2005. Information regarding the reception of remittances at the household level became available in the household surveys since 1997; this information enables us to assess the impact of remittances on the distribution of household per-capita income. Initially, the decomposition shown in column (3) shows a limited impact of non-labour income on inequality changes. This impact is broken down in column (4) into remittances, on the one hand, and other non-labour income (government transfers, capital incomes and other private transfers) on the other. At a country level and in rural areas, the impact is almost nonexistent, while in urban areas, the impact is slightly disequalizing.

1.2.3 Third sub-period: Inequality decrease (2005-2007) – recovery of the tradable sector, equalizing remittances and expanding social transfers

The period between 2005 and 2007 is characterized by a strong equalization in the household per-capita income distribution with a decrease by 5.2 Gini points at the country level, and by 7.3 and 3.2 Gini points in rural and urban areas, respectively. It is worth noting that changes in labour earnings and non-labour income are responsible, almost in equal proportions, for the equalization pattern observed at the country level during this period. However, labour earnings, as a driver for reducing inequality, appear to be more relevant in rural areas than in urban areas. On the other hand, non-labour income are extraordinarily equalizing in all areas explaining about 43% of the equalization in rural areas and about 80% in urban areas.

What explains the equalizing effect of labour markets? Why are they now producing more equity after having done the opposite in previous periods? The period between 2005 and 2007 is characterized by the commodity boom that also affects Honduras' main exports, coffee and bananas (Appendix, Figure A.1), thereby improving conditions in the tradable sector for the first time.

By decomposing the equalizing impact of non-labour income per adult, we are able to assess the impact of remittances on inequality. Columns 4 and 5 show that non-labour income accounts for 51% of equalization and that almost 44% of this equalization can be attributed to remittances, almost 25% to private transfers and capital incomes, and almost 12% to government transfers. The association between the aforementioned proximate determinants tends to disequalize the household per-capita income distribution diminishing, to some extent, the equalizing trend, suggesting that government transfers and private transfers, while both being equalizing on their own, increase inequality due to the rising association between them. Remittances have a stronger impact in rural areas, but the net impact, considering the association between the distribution of remittances and other-non-labour income, is almost the same in both areas (about 30%).

With respect to the impact of remittances, Figure 1.5 shows the evolution of the amount of per-capita remittance receipts by total household income quantile using an index (2002=100). Remittances across income quantiles do not exhibit any clear pattern until 2004, which explains why remittances had no equalizing or disequalizing effect.

On the contrary, starting from this year, the poorest seem to have benefited disproportionately from remittances (both in the number of beneficiaries among the poor as well as absolute amounts), leading to falling non-labour inequality as shown above.

Regarding policy changes, the period between 2005 and 2007 is of extraordinary interest due to the political transition that occurred in Honduras at the beginning of 2006, when the government switched from a centre-right conservative political party, headed by Ricardo Maduro, towards a left-wing populist inspired government led by Manuel Zelaya. In particular, cash transfer policies are critical here. Already in the early 1990s, a government conditional cash transfer program (PRAF) was created to minimize the undesirable effects produced by the neo-liberal adjustment programs implemented during the 1990s.

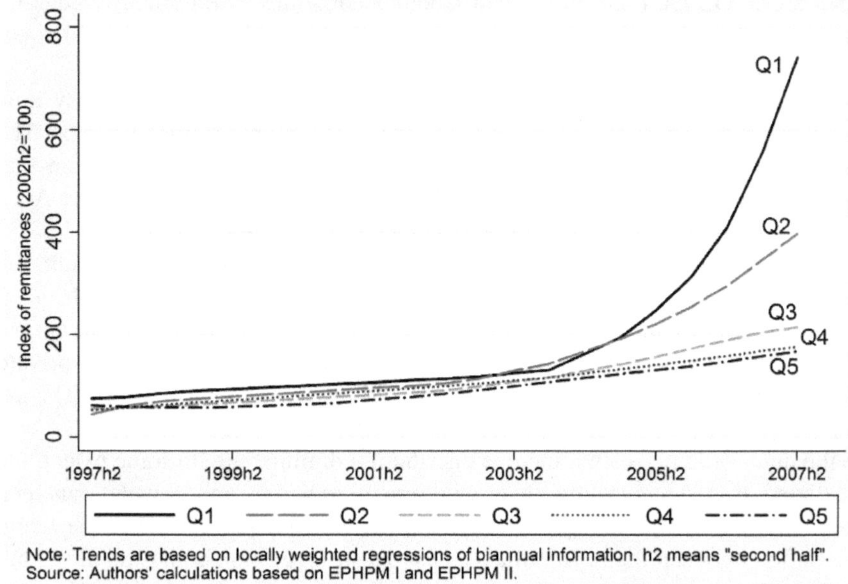

Figure 1.5: Index of remittances across quantiles of the total per-capita household income, 1997-2007

The first version of the program (PRAF-I) was implemented between 1992 and 1998. The Inter-American Development Bank (IADB) criticized PRAF-I for its leakage and poor targeting, as well as for ignoring supply side weaknesses (Moore, 2008). An adjusted program, PRAF-II was launched in 1998, being better targeted to rural areas. The program was aimed to support areas with the weakest infrastructure in the country. This design considered the supply-side incentives more importantly. It appears that the rural poor were still underrepresented in the beneficiary composition (Moore, 2008).

A third IADB loan program was launched under Zelaya's government in 2007 (PRAF-III).[34] His government aimed to adapt existing components and to create new ones, to fight low levels of human capital and chronic poverty. In-

[34] It may be argued that this credit was possible because Honduras reached the HIPC (Heavily Indebted Poor Countries) completion point and benefit from the MDRI (Multilateral Debt Relief Initiative) in 2006.

deed, previously existing PRAF components had not been able to solve these problems.[35] Conclusions from previous experiences were taken into account when designing the new program, particularly regarding the targeting of extremely poor households and the amount of transfers. During Zelaya's government, approximately 18-20 per cent of PRAF expenditure was transferred to extreme poor rural households (Moore, 2008). In Table 1.5, Zelaya's approach to transfers can be clearly distinguished from today's (2011) policies and those from 2005 and 2006 in terms of scope and transferred amounts per beneficiary.

Table 1.5: Basic Data on Conditional Cash Transfer programme (PRAF), selected years

	2005	2006	2007	2008	2011
Total number of beneficiaries	628,476	566,977	672,619	969,744	436,000
Total investment (1000 *Lempiras*)	407,706	370,009	573,527	639,517	313,830
Total investment (Mio. current US$)	21.6	19.6	30.3	33.8	16.5
Investment per beneficiary (current US$)	34.3	34.5	45.1	34.9	37.8

Source: Based on PRAF and Ministry of Finance (n.d.).

Table 1.6 shows how the structure of income changed considerably between 2005 and 2007. While labour incomes became less important, non-labour income grew substantially, mainly because of a considerable increase in government transfers, followed by remittances. Consistent with Table 1.4, social policy was starting to have an impact on inequality; but the scope of the program appears to have been cut back since then as shown in Table 1.5.

Even when the IADB loan contributed towards significantly expanding the PRAF programs, the impact on inequality depended on the targeting design and the implementation of the transfers. Barros' decomposition gives us information regarding both issues.

Our results show that the contribution of government transfers appears to equalize the income distribution; however, their rising association with other non-labour income cancelled out this impact. This means, that even when government transfers are, for the most part, equalizing, they are received mainly by households, which increasingly also rely on other non-labour income sources such as remittances, private transfers and capital incomes.

In summary, non-labour income was strongly equalizing the income distribution at the country level, driven by the rising equalization of remittances, private transfers, and government transfers. When examining rural and urban areas separately, labour incomes are much more important drivers of equalization in

35 For more information about the PRAF components, outcomes and expenditures see Moore (2008).

rural areas while in urban areas, remittances and other transfers play a relatively larger role. Government transfers also contribute towards equalization in both areas, but the impact remains modest.

Table 1.6: Income categories, 2005 and 2007 (in Lempiras of 1999)

	Amount		Structure	
Income categories	2005	2007	2005	2007
Total per-capita labour incomes	680.39	787.74	78.49	76.71
Total per-capita non-labour income	186.50	239.16	21.54	23.29
Government transfers (mainly PRAF)	45.12	63.02	5.20	6.14
Remittances	90.16	112.55	10.40	10.96
Other income (private transfers & capital incomes)	50.58	63.33	5.84	6.17

Source: Authors' calculations based on EPHPM I and EPHPM II.

1.3 Micro-econometric decomposition II: Determinants of changes in labour income inequality

As illustrated in our previous decomposition, changes in the distribution of labour incomes are by far the greatest contributor to the disequalization of the household per-capita income distribution between 1991 and 2005, particularly at the country level and in rural areas where most of the inequality change took place.[36] For this reason, by using another decomposition technique, we analyze inequality changes of labour earnings more thoroughly.

Table 1.7 shows that inequality in labour earnings rose by more than 7% between 1991 and 1999, and then again, by 4.5% between 1999 and 2005. In the two years that followed, labour inequality decreased by more than 3%. Gini coefficients for urban and rural areas show very different behaviours over time. Changes in inequality seem to be extremely accentuated in rural areas, while there are no significant trends in urban areas. Table A.3 in the Appendix shows rates of pro-poor growth in labour earnings observed during the periods between 1991-1999, 1999-2005 and 2005-2007. Earning changes were biased against the poor between 1991 and 2005, while in the subsequent period (2005-2007) they were strongly pro-poor. Changes in the slope of the growth incidence curves are mainly driven by what happened within low-earners (vulnerable) in rural areas.

36 According to household survey data, about 94%, 88%, 78.5% and 76.7% of the household per-capita income have been generated through labour activities in 1991, 1999, 2005 and 2007 respectively.

Table 1.7: Gini coefficient changes - monthly labour earnings distribution

Period	Whole country	Urban areas	Rural areas
1991	50.80	49.08	49.15
1999	54.52	49.99	55.13
Change	7.3%	1.9%	12.2%
1999	54.52	49.99	55.13
2005	57.00	49.46	60.88
Change	4.5%	-1.1%	10.4%
2005	57.00	49.46	60.88
2007	55.01	49.19	55.88
Change	-3.5%	-0.5%	-8.2%

Source: Authors' calculations based on EPHPM I and EPHPM II.

Many different forces exist behind the long-run changes in income distributions or, more generally, distributions of economic welfare within a population. Some of these forces have to do with changes in the distribution of factor endowments and socio-demographic characteristics, while others have to do with the returns these endowments produce and others with changes in the populations' behaviour such as labour supply, consumption patterns or the decision of whether or not to have children. These forces are not independent from each other. This is what makes it difficult to identify fundamental causes and mechanisms behind the dynamics of income distribution.

Decomposition techniques are used to identify drivers of distributional changes. Traditional techniques explain differences in scalar summary measures of distributions rather than in full distributions. The best known of these techniques is the Oaxaca-Blinder decomposition of differences in mean incomes across population groups with different characteristics (Blinder, 1973; Oaxaca, 1973) and the variance-like decomposition property of the so-called decomposable summary inequality measures (Bourguignon 1979; Cowell 1980; Shorrocks 1980). To assess the relevance of the various factors on income inequality changes, handling whole distributions instead with averages, a micro-econometric decomposition methodology first proposed by Bourguignon et al. (1998) was adjusted and applied to the Honduran case.[37] In particular, we will concentrate principally on returns to education and changes in education structure at the individual and household level, as well as changes in the returns to

[37] Variants of the basic methodology have been applied in Altimir et al. (2000), Bourguignon et al. (2001), Gasparini et al. (2005), Legovini et al. (1998) and Ferreira and Paes de Barros (1998), amongst others. See the basics of this decomposition in the Appendix. See also Bourguignon and Ferreira (2005).

occupations and sectors, which reflect the shifts between tradable and non-tradable sectors.[38]

1.3.1 Estimation strategy

Changes in inequality are always dependent on the years being compared. For this reason, it is crucial to provide reasons for the selection of years. We decided to decompose changes in Gini of labour incomes for the periods comprised between 1991 to 1999, 1999 to 2005 and 2005 to 2007. We include 1991 and 2007 because we want to have the broadest possible perspective that our data allows. We additionally include 2005 because, as shown above, this is where labour income inequality reaches its peak. Through the inclusion of this turning point in the decomposition, it is possible to study the determinants of the equalization, rather than the disequalization of the labour income distribution. We include 1999 in the decomposition because it offers the possibility to control for the impact of the 1998 Hurricane Mitch on the labour income distribution.

Let β be the vector of parameters determining market hourly earnings and λ the vector of parameters affecting employment outcomes (hours of work and participation). In order to estimate the equations for earnings and working hours, it is necessary to estimate the vector parameters β and λ. Since we do not have a socio economic panel survey for Honduras, we have to rely on a procedure which allows to replicate the structure of observed and unobserved characteristics of the year t into the year t_2 and vice versa.

H_i is the number of working hours by worker i and w_i indicates the hourly earnings received by the same individual. In a process of utility maximization, H_i is the optimal number of working hours, being determined based on market conditions. Heckman (1974) states that it is possible to derive an estimable reduced form, starting from a structural system obtained from a utility maximization problem of labour-consumption decisions. Individuals allocate hours to work and leisure to maximize their utility given their wealth, earnings, time and other constraints. The solution to this problem of maximization can be characterized as consumption and leisure functions given relevant prices.

Under general conditions, it is possible to invert these functions to obtain prices and labour incomes as functions of consumed quantities and worked hours. In particular, the earnings obtained in this way (w^*) can be interpreted as marginal valuations of labour, which are a function of personal characteristics,

38 Note that our methodology allowed us to control for composition effects of factors not subject to structure simulation. Composition effects are implicitly considered in the contribution of changes in working hours.

hours worked (amongst others) and represent the minimum wage for which the individual would work for a determined number of hours. On average, if the individual decides to work, the number of hours worked should be equal to their marginal value w* with the wage effectively received. Conversely, an individual decides not to go to work if the marginal value is greater than the wage offered.

Consequently, our model consists of two equations; one for hourly earnings (w*) and one for the number of worked hours (H*). These equations are a function of exogenous vectors taken as given, affecting earnings (X_1) and hours of work (X_2), which are allowed to have elements in common. The equation for working hours includes composition variables, which will reflect in the simulated working hours, compositional changes, or in other words, changes between the relative size of sectors, occupations, etc.[39]

Under this framework, the error terms ε_1 and ε_2 represent unobservable factors, which affect the determination of endogenous variables. In order to specify our model, for individual i, we observe positive values for w* and H* only if the individual actually works; if not, we only know that the reservation wage is higher than the offered one:

$$W_I^* = X_{1i}\beta + \varepsilon_{1i} \qquad i = 1, \dots, N \qquad (6)$$

$$H_i^* = X_{2i}\lambda + \varepsilon_{2i} \qquad (7)$$

We then have the following observation rule:[40]

$$W_i = W_i^* \quad \text{if} \quad H_i^* > 0$$

$$W_i = 0 \quad \text{if} \quad H_i^* \leq 0$$

$$H_i = H_i^* \quad \text{if} \quad H_i^* > 0$$

$$H_i = 0 \quad \text{if} \quad H_i^* \leq 0$$

Regarding estimation issues, we assume that the terms ε_1 and ε_2 are bivariate normal distributed with $E(\varepsilon_{1i}) = E(\varepsilon_{2i}) = 0$ and variances σ_{12} and σ_{22} are correlated

39 Note that vector X_2 also contains variables indicating occupation, economic sector, regions, gender, wage work, current enrolment, marital status, employment status of other household members and urban/rural area.

40 Consistent with the data used for the estimation, observed wages for a nonworking individual are zero.

with correlation coefficient ρ. This specification corresponds to the Tobit type-3 model in Amemiya's classification.[41] Even though it is possible to estimate all the parameters using a full information maximum likelihood method, we adopted a limited information approach that has notable computational advantages. We estimate the hours of work equation by means of a Tobit type-1 model in Amemiya's classification in which the variable is observed only if it is positive. The parameters of interest can be estimated using a standard censored regression Tobit model.[42] In order to control for behavioural responses within the household, each simulation of hourly earnings and working hours requires conditional estimations for spouses conditional on the behaviour of the head of household, and for other household members conditional on heads and spouses.[43]

1.3.2 Returns to education

Figure 1.6 illustrates the evolution of the returns and relative supply of workers by educational levels and areas.[44] Returns to schooling increased slightly between 1991 and 1994;[45] however, between 1994 and 2005, returns to education declined substantially. Why did this trend take place?

Between 1991 and 1994, the demand for skills in rural areas outpaced the supply, which remained almost constant throughout this period. Consequently, the skill premium increased considerably during this period of real exchange rate devaluation. Subsequently, slowly rising supply (combined with stagnant or falling demand) appear to be driving the falling returns to education between 1995 and 2005. From 2005 onwards, returns to high levels of education increased even when a significant expansion of a higher level of education took place. In urban areas, the situation appears to be much simpler; declining returns are explained principally by the educational upgrade.

Looking at the results of the decomposition in Table 1.8, changes in the returns to education had an equalizing effect between 1991 and 2005 across the

---

41 See Amemiya (1985).

42 This strategy is consistent but not fully efficient. In any case, the efficiency loss is not necessarily significant for a small sample. Technical details about the estimation procedure are available upon request.

43 Each simulation represents a whole distribution of labour earnings; therefore, based on these simulated distributions, it is possible to obtain a variety of other inequality indexes. These can be provided upon request by the authors.

44 Returns are obtained from the Heckman ML wage regression (excluded category "without formal education").

45 This trend is also observed in Mexico; see López-Calva and Lustig (2010).

country. Then, the period between 2005 and 2007 is characterized by disequalizing returns in rural areas and (slightly) equalizing returns in urban areas. Why do we observe different patterns in urban and rural areas during this last period? We may find some explanation in the commodity boom mentioned before. The upsurge of the tradable sector (see Figure 1.3) could have increased the demand for skills in rural areas. However, we also need to study the impact of changing endowments to get a more complete picture.

1.3.3 Structure of education

The educational upgrading of the labour force may also have an impact on the distribution of earnings. For instance, there is evidence for Brazil, Mexico and Peru where improvements in the distribution of schooling attainment led to an equalization of the earnings distribution.[46] However, as documented in Bourguignon, Ferreira and Lustig (2005), the equalization in years of schooling may yield in the short run to disequalize the income distribution (dubbed the 'paradox of progress').

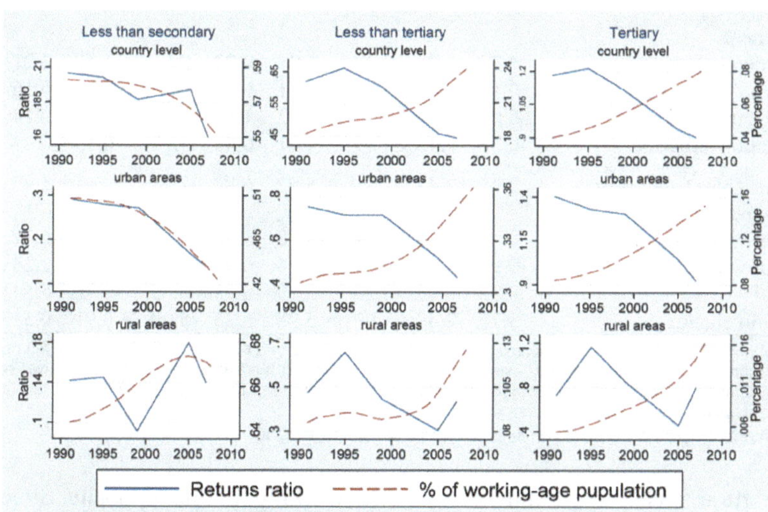

Note: Return ratios are relative to returns for those with no formal education. Different y-axis scales.
Source: Authors' calculations based on EPHPM I and EPHPM II.

Figure 1.6: Structure and returns to education, 1991-2007

46 López-Calva and Lustig (2010).

At least during the 1990s, we expect that the net flow of migrants from rural to urban areas disequalizes the urban distribution (see Table 1.3). Moreover, given the fact that in urban areas the educational upgrading is driven by an expanding tertiary education, we expect a strong disequalization due to changes in the structure of education. From 1999 onwards, a priori, it is difficult to predict a clear pattern regarding expected inequality changes. Even when the expansion of tertiary education speeds up, this effect is superseded by an extraordinary upgrading at the bottom of the distribution.

Table 1.8: Decompositions of the change in the Gini coefficient, labour earnings, selected periods

	Country level			Rural areas			Urban areas		
	1991-99	1999-2005	2005-07	1991-99	1999-2005	2005-07	1991-99	1995-2005	2005-07
Returns									
Individual education	-1.35	-1.24	0.62	-1.95	-1.44	1.69	-1.76	-1.29	-0.29
Household education	-0.34	-1.01	0.59	0.80	-1.09	0.35	-0.52	-1.20	0.33
Experience (potential)	-0.69	0.80	-0.10	-1.02	-0.85	0.62	-0.68	3.27	-0.62
Sectoral occupation	0.36	2.42	-1.52	8.06	2.82	-1.83	-0.15	0.87	0.11
Other	0.20	0.48	-0.48	1.27	0.48	0.00	-0.16	-1.08	0.22
Endowment									
Individual education	2.73	-0.75	-0.91	-5.91	-0.99	-3.67	1.48	-0.21	-1.24
Household education	-0.11	-0.18	-0.01	-0.11	-0.02	-0.09	-0.03	-0.16	-0.01
Experience (potential)	-0.01	-0.04	-0.03	-0.02	-1.15	-0.01	-0.04	-0.14	-0.03
Population structure	-0.28	-0.42	-0.09	0.21	-0.48	-0.13	-0.35	0.44	0.02
Unobservables (returns & endowments)	3.35	3.43	-2.31	5.92	6.89	-4.77	2.18	2.97	-0.88
Hours of work, intensity	0.42	-2.72	1.14	-3.78	3.30	0.15	2.66	-6.77	0.24
Hours of work, employment	-0.91	1.68	0.84	0.24	-0.95	1.98	-0.93	2.24	1.56
Residual	0.35	0.03	0.26	2.29	-0.78	0.72	-0.78	0.53	0.32
Total Gini change	3.72	2.48	-1.99	5.98	5.75	-5.00	0.91	-0.53	-0.27

Technical note: This table shows the average contribution to the observed Gini change produced by the observed change in each determinant. Averages come from changing the base year from t to t' (two earnings simulations required). See Bourguignon and Ferreira (2005). See Klasen et al. (2012) for a technical description of the model specification.

Source: Authors' calculations based on data from EPHPM I and EPHPM II.

In rural areas, structural changes are working in the opposite direction. While the expansion of tertiary education in rural areas is almost absent, improvements in the bottom tail of the skill distribution took place (albeit, slowly and insufficiently). Moreover, individuals placed on average at the extremes of the skill distribution are more likely to migrate to urban areas (see Table 1.3).[47] Consequently, changes in the structure of rural education, including rural-urban migration, are expected to equalize the rural distribution of earnings.

Decomposition results in Table 1.8 confirm this. Changes in the structure of education in urban areas were strongly disequalizing during the 1990s and also dominated country-level changes. In rural areas, as expected, changes in the structure of education were strongly equalizing for all three periods.

With both education endowments and returns pointing towards equalization in rural areas, other factors must have dominated these trends to produce the drastic increase in labour income inequality during the period 1991-2005.

1.3.4 Returns by sectors and occupations as well as sectoral change

In Table 1.8, we grouped the inequality impact on the labour income distribution caused by changes in returns to different economic sectors and occupations.[48] The combination of sectors and occupations yield a rich labour market division in many "sector-occupations" of different scopes, with a great number of workers such as agricultural labourers and very small groups, such as, for example, management staff in agriculture. Conditional to education and other covariates, our results show that in rural areas, the change in returns per sector-occupation is the main inequality driver during the 1990s and one of the most important drivers between 1999 and 2005. This finding empirically confirms the assumption that the labour income distribution becomes more unequal due to the evolution of the inter-sectoral earnings-gap taking place across the whole ability distribution. It supports the predictions by Devillanova et al. (2010) that if moving costs and skills are correlated and there is capital-skill complementarity, a trade-induced sectoral shift would increase wage inequality between different skill levels in a sector and within skill levels across sectors.

By comparing two groups of workers from different sector-occupations, it can clearly be seen how returns for specific sector-occupations are driving disequalization. Consider the first group of agricultural workers with less than secondary education (including those who never attended school). They earned, in

47 In rural areas, the upper tail of the skill distribution corresponds to those with at least a secondary education.

48 We identify the following four sectors: agriculture and related sub- sectors; manufacturing; financing, communication and personal services; and other sectors. The occupations are: professionals and technicians; directors; office workers; agricultural workers; drivers; manufacturing workers; transport workers; and service workers.

real terms, 28 and 30 *Lempiras* per hour in 1991 and 1999, respectively. A second group of workers in the finance, communication and services sector, with more than secondary education earned 75 and 111 *Lempiras* per hour, for the same respective years. While the first group increased their real hourly earnings by 8% in eight years, the second group's earnings increased by 48%. Note that the first group belongs typically to the more "traditional" agricultural sector, while the second group is part of the dynamic non-tradable sector.

In order to confirm the existence of a growing wage gap between the tradable and non-tradable sectors, we estimate hourly earnings for those with less than secondary education (including no school attendance). Returns to the tradable and the non-tradable sectors increased by 13% and 23% per hour, respectively, during the period 1991-1999. This means that, after controlling for education, working in the tradable sector makes a huge difference.

Table 1.8 also shows the impact of hours of work in different sectors and occupations (dubbed 'employment'), effectively modelling the impact of sectoral and occupational change, as well as hours within a sector (dubbed 'intensity'). The results show no clear and persistent trends in the country overall, or in urban and rural areas. This implies that inter-sectoral and occupational mobility has not been a major factor explaining inequality in labour earnings, supporting the claim of a relatively rigid labour market with little inter-sectoral mobility.

During the period 1991-1999, in rural areas the increasing demand for skills and the insufficient mobility of less-skilled workers determines an extraordinary dispersion of the returns across sectors and occupations. The fact that low-ability individuals in the expanding sector could work more intensively, can explain why changes in working hours help to partially compensate this disequalizing trend.[49]

Between 1999 and 2005, in rural areas the disequalization induced by changes in the returns to skills, sectors and occupations is reinforced by the impact of changes in the hours of work.[50] This effect can be attributed to the increasing demand for skilled labour in the dynamic sector, given the imperfect labour immobility constraining less-skilled workers to escape from the declining tradable sector. Consequently, this sector demands disproportionately less working hours by unskilled workers inducing high levels of underemployment.

This effect can be attributed to the increasing demand for skilled labour in the dynamic sector, given the imperfect labour immobility constraining less-skilled workers to escape from the declining tradable sector. Consequently, this

49 This is due to the complementarity between the two types of labour (skilled and unskilled).

50 Returns to skill consist of returns to formal education and unobserved ability.

sector demands disproportionately less working hours by unskilled workers inducing high levels of underemployment.

1.3.5 Unobservables

Many characteristics of workers and circumstances cannot be observed. Our methodology allows us to control for omitted variables. Motivation, ethnicity and soft skills, amongst others, may be behind significant changes in the distribution of earnings. Some of these could be a direct consequence of unobserved differences in quality of education or technological change affecting demand for unobservable skills.

During the 1990s, a technological change took place in Honduras during the liberalization phase. Operating new technologies requires skills, but the supply of highly-skilled labour was very limited. In such an environment (and given the problems of the education system), skills may be less related to formal education than to the (unobserved) ability to adapt to these new work environments in the modern non-tradable (e.g. high-end services) sectors. Given this, if a growing proportion of the valuable skill endowment is unobserved, the impact of unobservables on inequality represents nothing different than increasing returns to unobserved skills and the intensification of their use. The fact that something is unobservable does not mean that it does not exist. Therefore, because much more than half of the variance in wage rates or weekly earnings is explained by unobserved characteristics, it is also not surprising that the same factors are extremely relevant in explaining changes in labour income inequality.

Our results in Table 1.8 confirm the disequalizing role of unobserved characteristics between 1991 and 2005, most importantly in rural areas. However, how do unobservable characteristics transform into an equalizing force between 2005 and 2007? We could speculate that the upsurge of the tradable sector, mainly based on agricultural (rural) supply, thinned out the inter-sector wage gap, reducing the price of non-observed (modern) skills and increasing relative returns of old-fashioned (traditional) formal education. An interesting hypothesis would be that, on the one hand, the tradable sector demands relatively more traditional skills, highly correlated with years of education; while, on the other hand, the non-tradable sector demands, for instance, higher levels of soft skills (mostly uncorrelated with the poor rural education). This hypothesis finds support in our results as the effect on inequality of education and the unobserved ability work in opposite directions. Therefore, increasing profitability gaps between the tradable and non-tradable sectors may also intensify the disequalizing power of unobservable characteristics, and vice versa.

In order to investigate this issue, the final analytical section presents a methodology to assess the role of the tradable and non-tradable earnings gap in explaining inequality changes of labour incomes.

1.4 Micro-econometric decomposition III: Linking the microeconomic evidence to the macroeconomic story

In this section, we present a model for linking findings from the microeconometric decomposition above with the macroeconomic story. Our central argument regarding macroeconomic events and inequality trends was that the effects of trade liberalization in the 1990s, combined with a large inflow of remittances and donor capital, in response to the destruction caused by natural disasters, led to a highly overvalued currency that depressed the tradable sector. Adverse commodity prices and the destruction caused by Hurricane Mitch further damaged the agricultural exports considerably. The story changes during the mid-2000s as a consequence of higher commodity prices recovering the highly depressed labour incomes in the tradable sector.

The concept behind our model is that there is underemployment in the tradable sector, and labour-market segmentation restricts the access to the predominantly modern non-tradable sector. Consequently, a earnings-gap between both sectors emerges, depending on relative labour demand conditions and levels of productivity. In the tradable sector, given adverse international market conditions - such as depressed commodity prices and overvalued exchange rates – it may not pay to increase productivity in this sector and labour incomes will stagnate. In contrast, the same conditions will increase earnings and revenues in the non-tradable sector of investments there, which are also favoured by the external environment.

In this model, we assume workers' heterogeneity (allowing correlation between mobility costs and skills) causing an insufficient mobility of workers between tradable and non-tradable sectors (inducing a positive sloped non-tradable labour supply) and capital-skill complementarity. Therefore, different equilibrium labour incomes across sectors determine the observed earnings-gap between sectors. Note that this formulation is compatible with the model by Devillanova et al. (2010) which also relies on the complementarity between the two types of labour. The prediction of this formulation is that an economy suffering a sectoral shift against the backward sector will increase the inequality between and within sectors.

The key issue in this methodology is to decompose a distributional change of rural earnings (which is the sum of the tradable and non-tradable sectors) into two determinants. On the one hand, a "within-sector" determinant (*WS*), that is, a determinant of inequality changes which is not directly correlated with returns to the tradable and non-tradable sectors,[51] and on the other hand, a "between-sector" determinant (*BS*) which captures inequality changes due to variations in the relative returns to the sectors (given a fixed structure of endowments, their returns and the sectoral employment shares).[52]

The *BS* determinant captures the effect of a structural change in key macroeconomic variables. Given the structure of endowments (observed and unobserved), their returns and the employment shares by sectors, this determinant reflects the direct contribution to inequality changes from "macroeconomic" variables, which may alter the relative sector competitiveness.[53] For instance, a reduction of import barriers, an appreciation of the nominal exchange rate, an increasing public deficit, the non-adjustment of the obsolete or damaged export infrastructure and declining prices of commodities are only a few examples of institutional and market changes, partially driven by adverse climatic events, that can have an impact on the real exchange rate.

The impact of a change in the *BS* determinant can be depicted as a horizontal shift of the tradable or non-tradable labour earnings density function. Consequently, the rural labour income distribution changes its shape even when the sectoral density functions do not experience any change in their respective shapes or weights. Based on this decomposition idea, we present a methodology for decomposing the distributional change in a structural macroeconomic *BS* effect (earnings gap effect) and in a *WS* effect, as a result of changes in endowments, returns and employment intensity (including those caused indirectly by macroeconomic changes, see below). More formally, we propose an Oaxaca-Blinder type of decomposition, which can be illustrated as follows:

$$\Delta D = D(WS', BS') - D(WD, BS) \qquad (8)$$

51 Imagine that rural earnings are built-up by adding the tradable and non-tradable distributions. This determinant would reflect inequality changes that may arise by changes in the shapes and weights of both wage density functions.

52 The "between-sector" determinant captures inequality changes resulting from the horizontal shift of one or both wage density functions, keeping shapes and employment shares of the density function(s) constant.

53 However, such macroeconomic variables or events may also have an indirect contribution to inequality changes. This contribution works through affecting other relevant prices of the labour market. In this case, the indirect impact will be captured by the *WS* determinant (changes in the shape and shares of the sectoral density functions).

... where the second period is denoted by " ' ". The distributional change may be decomposed sequentially as follows:

$$\Delta D = [D(WS',BS') - D(W'D,BS)] + [D(WS',BS) - D(WD,BS)] \quad (9)$$

Equation (9) indicates that the distributional change may be decomposed in a earnings gap effect (between sectors) in t' and a within sectors effect as in t.[54] In order to perform the decomposition, we need to isolate the earnings gap change between sectors maintaining the shapes and employment shares of the sectoral earnings density functions constant. In other words, we need to find the maximal horizontal shift of the tradable labour income density function in t' which is consistent with the observed rural labour earnings density function in t.

More precisely, while holding the position of the non-tradable earnings density function unchanged as in t' we need to find and isolate the horizontal shift of the tradable earnings density function (from t' to t) which combined then with the change in the shape and employment levels of both sectoral labour earnings density functions from t' to t consistently simulate the whole rural distribution in t. or:

$$g = \min \{|g(q)|, \overline{WS'}\} \quad (10)$$

... where g stands for quantile and $g(q)$ is a function indicating the earnings gap change as a function of the quantile and $\overline{WS'}$ represents fixed endowments and returns in both sectors in t'. If the gap change is positive, then the minimum earnings gap change will disequalize the distribution of rural earnings; however, if the gap change is negative, then the minimum earnings gap change will equalize the distribution. Even when the solution of the above minimization problem may yield closed-form first-order and second-order conditions, in the case of non-monotonic earnings gap change functions, we rely in a non-parametric technique to find the solution.

By calculating and constructing sectoral Pen's parades, it is possible to derive a growth incidence curve of the between-sector earnings gap $g(q)$. Each Pen's parade is estimated for the tradable and non-tradable labour earnings distributions in t and t'. Figure 1.7 is a representation of the mentioned growth incidence curve for the three periods analyzed. Once g in the equation (10) is derived, we shift the tradable distribution by adding g to the entire distribution of

54 As we can see, there is no path dependence arising in this methodology. As ΔD is observed, the decomposition only requires an estimation of D(WS',BS). The BS effect can be easily calculated estimating the first term in equation (9).

earnings in the tradable sector in t'. Thus, we simulate $D(WS', BS)$ in (9), which is the simulated rural distribution with returns, endowment and shares as in t' and the earnings gap as in t. As we already know (WD, BS), which is the observed rural distribution in t, and $D(WS', BS')$, which is the observed rural distribution in t', it is possible to estimate equation (9), and decompose labour income inequality changes as mentioned.

One should emphasize that this method is likely to underestimate the complete impact of macro conditions on the sectoral distribution of labour incomes. In particular, one can well imagine that the macro conditions that caused a favourable shift towards the non-tradable sector not only shifted the entire earnings distribution to the right but also affected different portions of the distribution differently. For example, the shift towards non-tradables and the adverse shift from tradables might have worsened the employment conditions of poorly paid agricultural workers more than better paid workers in the tradable sector. In that sense, our analysis probably represents a lower bound.

We can now examine to what extent the gap in earnings between the two sectors is actually driving changes in the labour earnings distribution. In Figure 1.7 below, we show changes in the earnings gap between the tradable and non-tradable sectors by quantiles of the earnings distribution in rural areas. While changes in the shapes of the curves are also a consequence of changing returns to skills and employment levels in the two sectors, the minimum vertical shift of the curves can be understood as the contribution of the general shift of conditions favouring the tradable vs. the non-tradable sector. Between 1991 and 2005, this shift increases, widening the gap between the two sectors; between 2005 and 2007, however, the gap is shrinking.[55]

Table 1.9: The 'macroeconomic' (between sectors) earnings-gap effect on labour income inequality changes (using the Gini Index)

	Observed distributions		Simulation I sectors		Simulation II occupations		% of change			
							Sectors		Occupations	
	Rural	Country	Rural	Country	Rural	Country	Rural	Country	Rural	Country
1991	49.15	50.80	—	—	—	—	—	—	—	—
1999	55.13	54.52	54.95	54.24	54.73	53.98	3.06	7.53	6.74	14.52
2005	60.88	57.00	60.44	56.03	60.00	55.73	7.66	39.11	15.31	51.21
2007	55.88	55.01	56.50	55.68	56.66	55.60	-12.38	-33.67	-15.60	-29.65

Source: Authors' calculations based on data from EPHPM I and EPHPM II.

55 Using the above methodology, g is equal to 0.43, 0.14 and -0.14 log points for the periods 1999-1991, 2005-1999 and 2007-2005, respectively.

Table 1.9 shows the (minimum) contribution to inequality changes as a result of an exogenous change in the earnings gap between the tradable and non-tradable sectors (Simulation I - sectors) and between the tradable and non-tradable occupations (Simulation II - occupations).[56] As expected, the contribution to inequality changes of increasing conditional gaps being consistent with the observed inequality changes over time. In other words, given a structure of endowments, their returns and employment shares, an exogenous change favouring the non-tradable sector (occupation), yields to higher levels of labour earnings inequality and vice versa. Between 1991 and 1999, results show that the exogenous macroeconomic shift between the tradable and non-tradable sectors (occupation) explains a minimum of 7.5-14.5% of the observed disequalization at the country level, depending on the simulation.

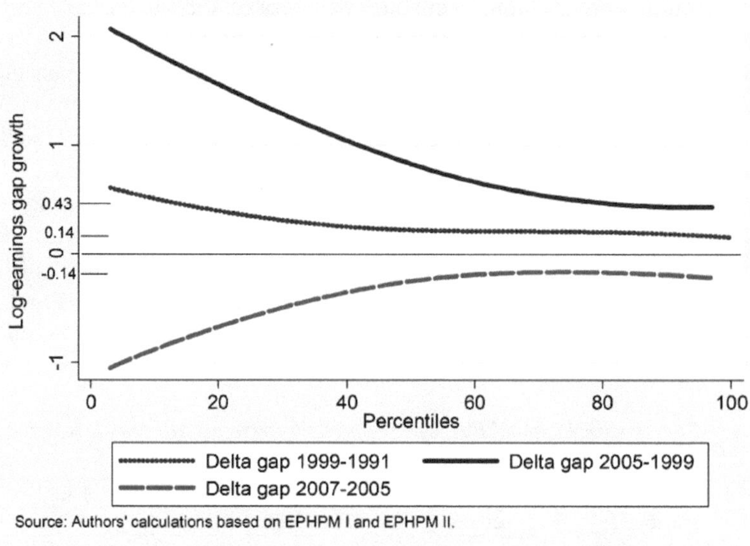

Figure 1.7: Growth incidence curves for the inter-sectoral earnings gap in rural areas

56 The tradable sector includes many occupations that are not directly related to trade activities (e.g. personnel transport in agriculture). On the other hand, tradable occupations include only occupations, which are directly related to trade activities (e.g. agricultural workers in the same sector). Here, the tradable occupation should narrowly reflect the consequences on inequality arising from changes in the relative Honduran export competitiveness.

The contribution tends to be higher in the later periods contributing up to 50% of the disequalization between 1999 and 2005. However, many other intra-sectoral and inter-occupational gaps exist, which are not controlled for. In this sense, our results point out the disequalizing effect of other occupational sorting, some of which was indirectly induced exogenously by trade, but some that could be related to other shifts in demand for different types of labour within the sectors. This finding suggests that the shifts between tradable and non-tradable sectors, plus structural shifts that increase the demand for unobservables, combined with structural rigidities in labour markets that limit mobility, combine to drive up labour earnings inequality between 1991 and 2005. Note that the effects are larger at the country level than in rural areas as the rural income distribution is at the bottom of the overall country distribution and a widening of it has a larger proportionate effect on the overall country distribution. After 2005, the commodity boom seems to have reversed the tradable-non-tradable shift, but whether it is able to overcome the other structural causes of rising inequality, is hard to predict at present.

1.5 Conclusions and remaining challenges

In Honduras, increasing income inequality throughout the last two decades has mainly been a rural phenomenon, occurring within a context characterized by a fall in demand for tradables (linked to an overvalued exchange rate) trade-induced skill-biased technological change and a low labour mobility between a shrinking and increasingly less dynamic tradable sector and the more dynamic non-tradable sector. A lack of policies oriented towards the promotion of exports, an appreciated real exchange rate, increasing flows of capital and more recently, remittances after Hurricane Mitch, have contributed towards supporting a trade deficit, encouraged by a disappointing performance of the commodity exports (coffee during the 1990s and bananas during the 2000s). All these elements establish the framework, which helps to explain the inequality increase during the 1990s and the first part of the 2000s.

A variety of decomposition methodologies were used to understand the determinants and drivers of observed income inequality changes. First, we implemented an extended methodology proposed by Barros et al. (2006), finding that distributional changes in labour incomes are a strong determinant of inequality changes in the household per-capita income. However, between 2005 and 2007, the decrease in inequality is a consequence of equalizing trends in labour as well as non-labour income; for changes in non-labour income, remittances played a significantly equalizing role. However, HIPC debt relief and the resulting increased social transfer policies of the Zelaya government played only a relatively small equalizing role.

Second, the use of a micro-econometric decomposition methodology, based on Bourguignon et al. (2005), helped to assess factors determining inequality changes in labour earnings between 1991 and 2007. Changes in unobservables (prices and endowments) and in the structure of education, together with a pronounced occupational sorting associated with an increasing productivity gap between the tradable and non-tradable sectors, represent the main drivers of the disequalization between 1991 and 2005. Regarding unobservable factors, it is plausible that the relative expansion of the non-agricultural sector during the 1990s, which demands a wider set of skills, is behind the extraordinary contribution of the unobservable to the increase in labour income inequality. Contrary to this, during the 2000s the equalizing contribution of changes in the structure of formal education, together with a recovery of the tradable sector - driven by favourable external conditions and improved export revenues - promoted equality by increasing earnings in the tradable sector, expressed as a reduction in the price to occupations (occupational sorting), and an equalizing impact of changes in unobservable factors on inequality.

We argue that the underlying determinant of the disequalization is the low mobility between sectors and occupations, where typically a poor agricultural worker is unable to abandon his sector and change to other sectors or occupations. As shown in our model, improvements in productivity tend to cancel the earnings-gap between the tradable and non-tradable sectors and also ensure higher labour income levels, while improvements in mobility between sectors leads to an accelerated decrease in this gap. We argue that the rising international competitiveness through policies promoting the productivity of the tradable sectors, at the expense of other sectors, increases the standard of living in the country, when compared with treating the other sectors equally.

Regarding the structure of education, and contrary to a general Latin American trend since the second half of the 1990s, where many countries were able to compensate the increasing negative impact of technological change in income inequality by having simultaneously achieved a more equal distribution of education, Honduras did not begin this compensation process until the mid-2000s. Additionally, we present evidence linking internal migration and labour income inequality changes. Based on a structural probability model, it was possible to estimate that the educational structure of migrants at the origin (1994), actually affects the structure of education in urban and rural areas. As a result, educational structure worsened in urban areas and improved in rural areas. Additionally, the impact of educational shifts in urban and rural areas at the country level are extremely disequalizing during the period between 1991 and 1999. Furthermore, a lack of income generation opportunities in rural areas - partly due to a depressed tradable sector - contributed to the formation of urban poverty ghettos encouraging high levels of criminality and prompting people to leave the country.

Our decomposition methodology supports the conclusions by Devillanova et al. (2010) suggesting a channel through which trade integration can affect the earnings inequality in a context of capital-skill complementarity and imperfect mobility of workers. The story that follows is that a shift towards the non-tradable sector increases the skill intensity and skill premium in this sector (observed and unobserved ability). This evolution regarding skill intensity and skill premium is backed up by our results regarding the impact of unobservables on inequality in a rural economy characterized by duality. At the same time, relative earnings for less-educated workers also increase in the dynamic sector compared to those in the tradable sector (due to the imperfect mobility). Consequently, skilled and unskilled workers now perform better in the non-tradable sector (relative to those in the tradable sector). In the same manner, the labour income distribution becomes more unequal due to the evolution of the inter-sectoral earnings gap taking place across the whole ability distribution. However, an important proportion of the inequality increases and resulting equalization in the earning distribution cannot be attributed to labour-market forces, but rather to changes in the relative competitiveness coming exclusively from macroeconomic conditions.

Given the fact that inequality is partly a consequence of declining rural tradable earnings and inter-sectoral and inter-occupation immobility, policies oriented towards increasing labour force mobility and productivity, together with encouraging the competitiveness of the tradable sector are highly recommended in order to achieve desirable social-economic outputs. Given that almost 80% of the extremely poor live in rural areas, most of them working in the agricultural sector, it is critical to increase smallholder competitiveness, including export promotion policies, an adjustment of the real exchange rate and investments in rural infrastructure. However, a more promising step towards increasing rural earnings equity in the long-run is to provide a non-segmented education with productive and non-discriminatory values in rural areas that reduces the friction costs associated to internal migration (between sectors, occupations, and geographic regions).

The observed decrease in inequality between 2005 and 2007 should not be misunderstood as an already guaranteed change from the previous disequalizing trend. The evolution of inequality will depend heavily on the impact of the current international crisis, commodity prices and the flow of remittances. Even if social policies have so far shown only a neutral impact on inequality, they should be reinforced, since their possible success offers a limited set of tools to partly overcome the purely exogenous character of inequality trends so far.

Essay 2 - Sectoral shifts and inequality. How to relate macroeconomic events to inequality changes[ii]

Abstract

This paper presents a way to explore how macroeconomic shifts may cause inequality changes. It is based on the backwardness observed in certain sectors in developing countries. It shows why highly dualistic economies tend to be more unequal than economies with flexible and integrated labour markets. Assuming that an inter-sectoral earnings gap exists, this methodology offers a lower bound estimate of the direct impact on inequality changes caused by macroeconomic changes that affects the relative competitiveness between the tradable and non-tradable sectors. The methodology aims to find the earnings gap change (in log units) taking place between two points in time, which is not dependent on the distribution of endowments, their returns (observed and unobserved) and on the sectoral employment shares. The decomposition methodology proves to be consistent under few assumptions (log normal distribution of earnings and inter-sectoral stochastic dominance) and was tested using observed and simulated data. We suggest a channel through which trade integration can affect labour income inequality in a context of capital-skill complementarity and imperfect mobility of workers supporting the findings by Devillanova et al. (2010). Since segmentation is the underlying disequalization condition, policies oriented to encourage labour mobility appear to be highly desirable in such economies to reduce inequality and fight poverty.

---

ii This work won the "Best Paper Award" in the Arnoldshain Seminar XI conference on “Migration, Development, and Demographic Change – Problems, Consequences, Solutions”, June 25 – 28, 2013, University of Antwerp, Belgium. International Society for Comparative Economic Studies. ISCES.

2.1 Introduction

Boeke (1953) describes the simultaneous existence of both a traditional and a modern economic sector in a colonial economy. The traditional sector is labour intensive, with insufficient levels of capital stock and labour division; it takes place in rural areas mostly in the form of small-scale agricultural activities. In contrast to this, the modern sector is based on capital-intensive industries and large-scale agricultural activities oriented towards international markets. It is also argued that the large-scale agricultural modern sector mostly favours foreign enterprises without affecting rural labour incomes and living standards.

The descriptions made by Boeke during the last century seem to be also experienced by many developing countries in Latin America. Acemoglu et al. (2001) argue that the Spanish and Portuguese colonization strategy consisted of establishing a complex trade system of monopolies and trade restrictions in order to maximize the extraction of resources from the colonies. Unfortunately, extractive institutions continue to exist (to use the terminology of Acemoglu and Robinson) and are reflected nowadays in many political systems in the developing world. Robinson (2010) states that political systems tend to generate inegalitarian forces if political power is concentrated amongst narrow elites. As a matter of fact, developing countries are usually dominated by non-consolidated forms of democracy, thus allowing institutions to encourage or sustain an unequal distribution of incomes.[57]

Cornia (2012) argues that the desired inequality reduction in South America was achieved through macro policies favouring the labour-intensive tradable sector, as well as through changes in labour market policies and institutions. However, highly dualistic economies are usually characterized by the lack of such policies supporting the tradable sector and as a result, the dual structure of the economy appears to be a sort of equilibrium based on labour vulnerability and underemployment.[58]

The main purpose of this work is to consider the existence of a backward sector as a disequalizing condition. It raises the question how to define sectors in a consistent way. Because of the possibility to establish linkages with macroeconomic variables, this paper explores the backwardness of the tradable sector, encompassed by the agricultural, mining, and manufacture sectors. The tradable

---

57 Contrary to this, the natural conjecture is that democracy would imply income redistribution toward the relatively poor. In fact, Cornia (2012) suggests that during the last twenty years, many Latin American countries experienced a return to and consolidation of democracy, which possibly affected income inequality through the introduction of more progressive policies.

58 See Klasen, Otter, and Villalobos Barría (2012) on Honduras over the last 20 years.

sector produces goods that could eventually be exported. The approach of this paper is based on the idea that rural areas are the natural space where backwardness may take place. Figure 2.1 shows the rural income distribution in Chile and Honduras, illustrating both a non-dualistic and a well-recognized dualistic economy, respectively. The Honduran case clearly shows that the tradable sector lags behind the non-tradable sector. In order words, at each percentile, it is possible to observe a positive earnings gap between the tradable and non-tradable sectors (first order stochastic dominance). Interestingly, the impact of the minimum wage appears to be less important in Honduras than in Chile. While in Chile, it contributes to back both distributions on its value, in Honduras, the minimum wage framework contributes to spread the distribution. According to the Honduran Secretary for Labour (SENAEH), the minimum daily wage in 2005 ranged between 61.26 and 97.77 *Lempiras* in the agricultural and financial sectors, respectively. This evidence raises the question regarding the role of the minimum wage as an equalization instrument.

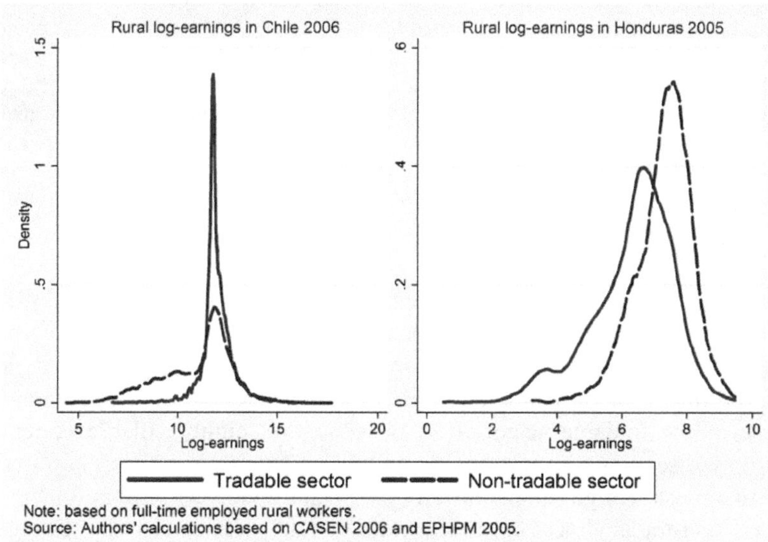

Figure 2.1: Non-dualistic and dualistic economies, Chile and Honduras in the mid 2000s

The tradable and non-tradable linkages to macro-economic variables have been studied in the literature. Agosin (2007) shows that the real exchange rates (RERs) in Latin American countries have been unstable, exhibiting strong cyclical fluctuation, associated to financial capital flows. This has proven to negatively affect the evolution of the tradable sector in terms of their volume (exports), diversification, and degree of integration of national economies. Ffrench-Davis (2011) argues that the highly cyclical evolution of RERs produces misaligned rates, affecting the volatility of the capital flows. Such volatility distorts investment decisions, promoting speculative and short-run investments, artificially displacing tradables (many produced by small- and medium-scale enterprises). Additionally, it discourages adding value to traditional exports, with regressive effects on employment and employment quality. Moreover, Damill and Frenkel (2012), using a panel OLS estimation with yearly data covering the period 1990-2010 for the 18 Latin American countries, find that depreciated real exchange rates (RERs) tend to significantly reduce unemployment (and also underemployment) with a time lag of two years.[59]

Ffrench-Davis (2011) argues that profound adjustments in the exchange policy are required and states:

> "Neoliberal views tend to state any exchange intervention involves going against the market, and that this is always defeated by that market. On the contrary, it is about an alternative approach, to achieve the real market forces – export producers and importers, and the producers of importable goods – who are the key players for productive development and equity, should prevail in determining the exchange rate. This is the market that must prevail, and not the market of short-term operators and rent seekers instead of innovation creators and greater productivity. To achieve this consistent and selective intervention by the economic authority is fundamental, and of course is not free of flaws."

Besides the economic policy aspects, other macro forces are behind the dual equilibrium, such as in the case of Honduras. For instance, natural catastrophes, destroying the rural stock of capital, contribute to sustain low productivity levels in the traditional sector. Commodity prices may also affect the relative competitiveness of the tradable sector. It is possible that highly volatile commodity prices may discourage investment in the tradable sector increasing non-tradable competitiveness. Knight and Johnson (1997) find evidence on this for the tradable and non-tradable sectors in Australia. Trade policies can also change the relative competitiveness of the tradable sector. Trade frameworks that do not

[59] Damill and Frenkel (2012) estimate an equation that is a variant of Okun's law and takes into account the influence of the RER on the employment-output ratio. The estimations included fixed country-effects to control for the continually diverging levels in national poverty and unemployment rates that are caused by differences in the measurement and definitions as well as in the labour market structures. The estimations also included fixed time-effects controlling for the external shocks.

take into account rural backwardness can also accelerate the expansion of import-related sectors and the non-tradable sector. Finally, exogenous capital shocks should be also considered; in particular, aid flows after catastrophes and remittances. These factors are relatively important for small economies. In the same way, Dutch Disease types of impacts are also expected in medium-sized economies due to highly competitive industries. For example, Ruehle and Kulkarni (2011) find that the Copper boom actually contracted the Chilean economy. As expected, such events would increase the gap showed in Figure 2.1 for the Honduran case, and consequences would be expected on the income inequality.

This paper will explore a methodology for isolating the impact on inequality changes produced directly by changes in the relative competitiveness of the tradable sector (instrumented as the earnings gap across quantiles between the tradable and non-tradable sectors). However, one should emphasize that this method is likely to underestimate the complete impact of macro conditions on the labour earnings distribution. In particular, one can well imagine that the macro conditions that caused a favourable shift towards the non-tradable sector not only shifted the entire earnings distribution to the right but also affected different portions of the distribution differently by changing relevant prices in the labour market.

This paper is broken down as follows: Section 2.2 reveals a theoretical model supporting the linkage between macroeconomic events and inequality changes, while Section 2.3 presents an illustration using simulated data. Section 2.4 offers a description of the proposed methodology. An application using real and simulated data is presented in Section 2.5, while Section 2.6 concludes this study.

2.2 Tradable and non-tradable sectors in the rural economy

Consider the rural economy consisting of two sectors: the tradable sector and the non-tradable sector. The tradable sector consists of agriculture, manufacture and mining. The non-tradable sector comprises all other economic activities. In this "*classical*" model, the tradable sector has an "*unlimited*" labour supply at the subsistence wage S available because there is an excess supply of unskilled labour, such that real earnings remain unchanged over time.

The non-tradable sector (or at least a significant portion of it) develops more sophisticated activities, which require a higher level of skills; this consequently does not often appeal to individuals in the subsistence sector since, according to

Lewis (1954), these will be forced to abandon / relinquish the carefree / easy-going way of life of the subsistence sector.[60] The non-tradable sector on average requires higher skills than the tradable sector so that the non-tradable sector has to pay a higher wage *W* which is typically higher than the subsistence wage *S*. Moreover, this model assumes inter-sectoral imperfect mobility; this means that only a few workers of the tradable sector may quit their work and compete for a job in the non-tradable sector. For this reason, we observe a positive-sloped labour supply in the non-tradable sector. If the non-tradable sector increases the proportion of workers, it has to pay progressively higher wages over the labour supply line. Figure 2.2 shows the main features of the model.

In this model, the wage gap and the underlying underemployment are considered a function of the relative competitiveness of the tradable sector. Regarding this issue, Lewis (1954) argues:

> "Owners of plantations have no interest in seeking knowledge of new techniques or new seeds conveyed to the peasants, and if they are influential in the government, they will not be found using their influence to expand the facilities for agricultural extension."

Besides the possibility that plantation owners behave as Lewis states, the context of low profit levels, high depreciation rates, overvaluation of the real exchange rate and volatile international commodity prices can contribute to explain why developing countries evolve in such a dual equilibrium. In the context of an extremely unskilled labour force, the optimal profit strategy can be focused on exploiting cheap labour without an interest in increasing labour productivity levels in the tradable sector.

Higher commodity prices or improved rural education may be seen as an upward shift in the marginal product of the tradable labour curve. High levels of inter-sectoral mobility can contribute to reach in the rural economy the famous "turning point" (see Lewis, 1954). This would induce a positive sloped labour supply in the tradable sector. So that increasing productivities in the non tradable sector, may translate into declining shares of labour in the tradable sector with less underemployment. From here onward, the classical assumption of unlimited labour supply ceases to hold. As a consequence of this, the wage gap will decrease. In the same way, low levels of inter-sectoral mobility determine that productivity improvements in the non-tradable sector will produce an increase in the wage gap.

---

60 Lewis (1954, p. 150) makes reference to the rural sector in contrast to the urban or modern sector.

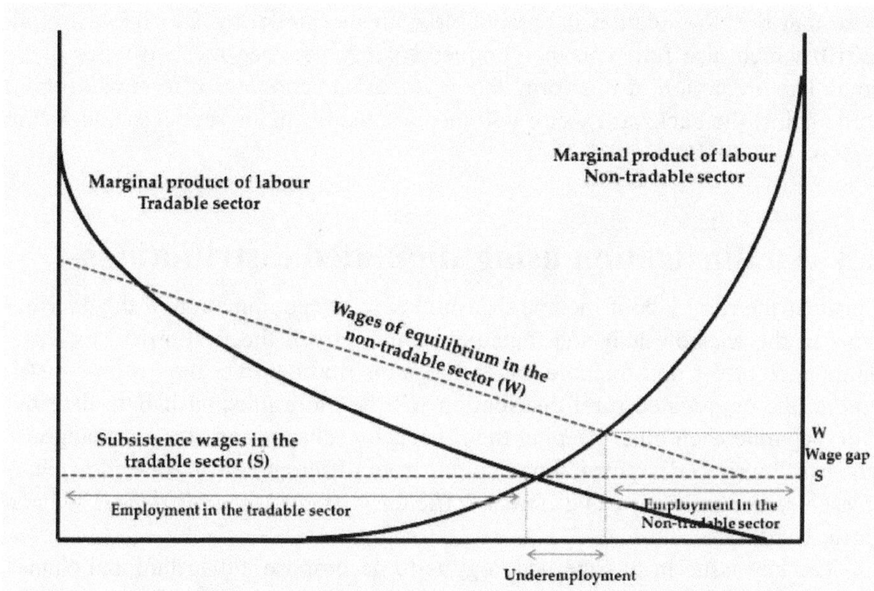

Figure 2.2: The labour market between the tradable and non-tradable sectors

This is only possible because workers in the tradable sector are unable to abandon this sector and represent an "*unlimited*" labour supply at the subsistence wage. The underlying force here is the inter-sectoral immobility encouraged by dualistic educational systems.

In summary, the concept behind this model is that there is underemployment in the tradable sector, and labour-market segmentation restricts the access to the predominantly modern non-tradable sector. Consequently, a wage gap between both sectors emerges, depending on relative labour demand conditions and levels of productivity. In the tradable sector, given adverse international market conditions – such as depressed commodity prices and overvalued exchange rates – it may not pay to increase productivity in this sector and wages will stagnate. In contrast, the same conditions will increase relative wages and revenues in the non-tradable sector of investments, which are also favoured by the external environment.

In this model, we assume workers' heterogeneity (allowing correlation between mobility costs and skills) causing an insufficient mobility of workers between tradable and non-tradable sectors (inducing a positive sloped non-tradable labour supply) and capital-skill complementarity. Therefore, different equilibrium wages across sectors determine the observed wage gap between sectors.

Note that this formulation is compatible with the model by Devillanova et al. (2010) which also relies on the complementarity between the two types of labour. The prediction of this formulation is that an economy suffering a sectoral shift against the backward sector will increase the inequality between and within sectors.

2.3 An illustration using simulated distributions

Consider the rural labour income distribution as the combination of the distributions in the tradable and non-tradable sectors. Given the first-order stochastic dominance of the non-tradable log-earnings distribution over the tradable distribution, the aggregated rural distribution will be more unequal if both distributions separate each other keeping their respective shapes and sizes unchanged.[61] The earnings gap described above comes from different skill price-endowments in each sector expressed as different "efficiency wages" (see Mirrlees, 1975 and Basu, 1984).

The key issue in this methodology is to decompose a distributional change of rural earnings into two determinants. On the one hand, a "*within-sector*" determinant (*WS*), that is a determinant of inequality changes, which is not directly correlated with returns to the tradable and non-tradable sectors,[62] and on the other hand, a "*between-sector*" determinant (*BS*), which captures inequality changes due to variations in the relative returns to the sectors (given a fixed structure of endowments, returns and sectoral employment shares).[63]

To illustrate the fundamentals of this methodology, consider that the graphs in Figure 2.3 were obtained based on the generation of two normal random distributions, assuming sectoral sizes and distributional moments observed in Honduras in 2005.[64] They represent the tradable and non-tradable sectors of the rural economy.

61 Klasen, Otter, and Villalobos Barría (2012) show evidence on this for Honduras.

62 This determinant would reflect inequality changes that may arise from changes in the shapes and sizes of both earnings density functions.

63 The "between-sector" determinant captures inequality changes resulting from the horizontal shift of one or both wage density functions, keeping the shapes of their density function constant.

64 Based on the Honduran specification, the simulation assumes that the tradable sector accounts for the 72% of the employment in rural areas. Urban and rural areas account for 51.6% and 48.4% of the employment respectively. All parameters for the simulated distribution were estimated based on EPHPM 2005.

The top-right graph shows the same distributions depicted in the top-left graph with the only difference that the whole tradable distribution is horizontally "displaced" to the left in one log unit, thus inducing an "artificial" earnings gap between sectors. It is additionally assumed that the *WS* determinant does not exist (implying that the shapes and sizes of both density distributions remain unchanged). The bottom panels show the rural distributions obtained by merging the random distributions directly above.

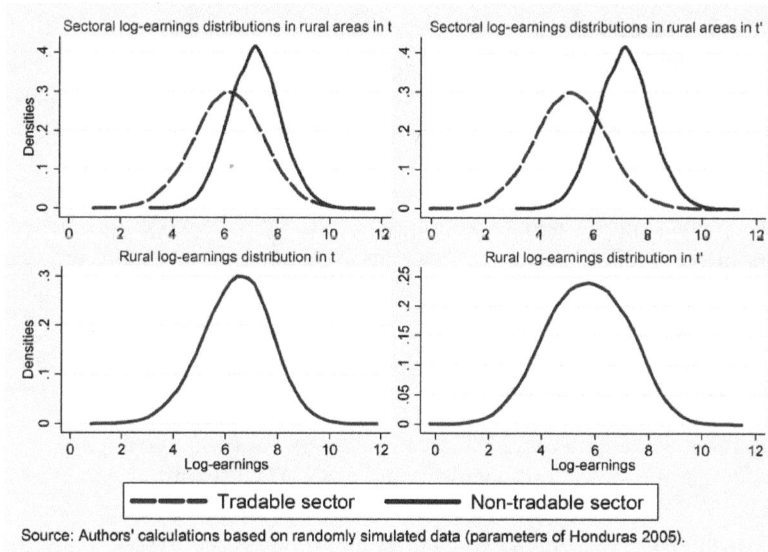

Figure 2.3: Inter-sectoral earnings-gap and inequality in rural areas

It is possible to see that the bottom-left distribution is more equal than its counterpart on the right. In order to estimate effects at the country level, a single urban log-earnings distribution is considered. It was generated also based on the distributional moments observed in the Honduran labour market in 2005.

Table 2.1 shows the (minimum) contribution to inequality changes as a result of an exogenous change in the earnings gap of one log-unit between the tradable and non-tradable sectors. Given a structure of endowments and their returns, an exogenous change favouring backwardness of the tradable sector yields to higher levels of labour earnings inequality and vice versa.

Table 2.1: The macroeconomic (between sectors) earnings-gap effect on labour income inequality changes (Gini Index) due to a one unit log earnings-gap shift

	Gini coefficient in *t*		Gini coefficient in t'		Gini change (t-t')	
Area	Mean	Sd.	Mean	Sd.	Points	Percentage
Rural	62.40	0.0029	68.20	0.0024	5.86	9.40
Country	60.29	0.0019	65.28	0.0017	5.02	8.33

Note: Each distribution consists of 100,000 observations.

Source: Authors' calculations based on 100 Gini simulations of distributions randomly generated.

Here, the impact is easily to observe because the simulation explicitly holds returns to endowments, endowments and sectoral employment shares constant (shapes unchanged). However, in the real economy, everything changes. Macroeconomic conditions contribute to change returns, and these changes affect the path of endowment accumulation. In highly dualistic economies, a shift towards non-tradables and the adverse shift from tradables might have worsened the employment conditions of poorly paid agricultural workers more than better paid workers in the tradable sector. In that sense, our analysis probably represents a lower bound of the impact of macroeconomic conditions on inequality changes.

2.4 The methodology

Based on this decomposition idea, a methodology for decomposing the distributional change in a structural macroeconomic *BS* effect (earnings gap effect) and in a *WS* effect is presented, as a result of changes in endowments, returns and employment shares by sectors (including those caused indirectly by macroeconomic changes, see below). More formally, we propose an Oaxaca-Blinder type of decomposition, which can be illustrated as follows:

$$\Delta D = D(WS', BS') - D(WD, BS) \qquad (1)$$

... where the second period is denoted by " ' ". The distributional change may be decomposed sequentially as follows:

$$\Delta D = [D(WS', BS') - D(W'D, BS)] + [D(WS', BS) - D(WD, BS)] \qquad (2)$$

Equation (2) indicates that the distributional change may be decomposed in an earnings gap effect (between sectors) in t' and a within sectors effect as in t.[65] In order to perform the decomposition, we need to isolate the labour earnings gap change between sectors maintaining the shapes and weights of the earnings density functions constant. In other words, we need to find the maximal horizontal shift of the tradable earnings density function in t' which is consistent with the observed rural labour income density function in t. More precisely, while holding the position of the non-tradable labour income density function unchanged as in t' we need to find and isolate the horizontal shift of the tradable labour earnings density function (from t' to t) which combined then with the change in the shape and the weights of both sectoral earnings density functions from t' to t consistently simulate the whole rural distribution in t. or:

$$g = min\,\{|g(q)|, \overline{WS'}\} \qquad (3)$$

... where g stands for quantile and $g(q)$ is a function indicating the earnings gap change as a function of the quantile and $\overline{WS'}$ represents fixed endowments, returns and employment shares in both sectors in t'. If the earnings gap change is positive, then the minimum earnings gap change will disequalize the distribution of rural labour incomes; however, if the gap change is negative, then the minimum gap change will equalize the distribution. Even when the solution of the above minimization problem may yield closed-form first-order and second-order conditions, in the case of non-monotonic earnings gap change functions, we rely in a non-parametric technique to find the solution. By calculating and constructing sectoral Pen's parades, it is possible to derive a growth incidence curve of the between-sector earnings gap $g(q)$. Each Pen's parade is estimated for the tradable and non-tradable labour earnings distributions in t and t'. Once g in the equation (3) is derived (in the simulation above g equals the unity), we shift the tradable distribution by adding g to the entire distribution of earnings in the tradable sector in t'. Thus, we simulate $D(WS', BS)$ in (2), which is the simulated rural distribution with returns, endowments and employment shares as in t' and the earnings gap as in t. As we already know (WD, BS), which is the observed rural distribution in t, and $D(WS', BS')$, which is the observed rural distribution in t', it is possible to estimate equation (2), and decompose labour inequality changes as mentioned.

65 As we can see, there is no path dependence arising in this methodology. As ΔD is observed, the decomposition only requires an estimation of $D(WS', BS)$. The BS effect can be easily calculated estimating the first term in equation (9).

2.5 An application using observed and simulated data

The application using observed data is taken from Klasen et al. (2012). Figure 2.4 shows three growth incidence curves of the earnings gap or gap(q) observed in Honduras during the periods 1991-1999, 1999-2005 and 2005-2007. In this set up, $g = \min\{|g(q)|, \overline{WS'}\}$ is equal to 0.14, 0.43 and -0.14 log units for the three periods respectively.

The simulated data is based on the distributional moments observed in Honduras in 1999 and 2005. Assuming that is g is equal to 0.43, $D(WS', BS)$ is simulated. Table 2.2 shows the contribution of the *BS* determinant to the inequality change using simulated data.

As expected, the contribution to inequality changes of increasing conditional gaps being consistent with the observed inequality changes in Honduras over time.[66] Between 1991 and 1999, results show that the exogenous macroeconomic shift between the tradable and non-tradable sectors explains a minimum of 7.5 percent of the observed disequalization at the country level.

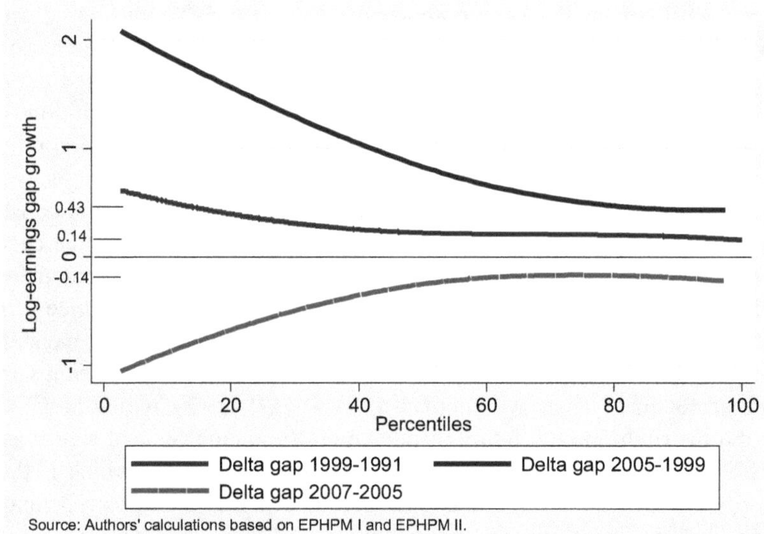

Figure 2.4: Honduran growth incidence curves of the inter-sectoral earnings-gap in rural areas

66 See Klasen et al. (2012).

Table 2.2: The macroeconomic (between sectors) earnings-gap effect on labour income inequality changes (Gini Index), simulated data

	Observed distributions		Displaced distributions		Percentage change	
Year	Rural	Country	Rural	Country	Rural	Country
1999	56.73	56.54	-	-	-	-
2005	62.40	60.29	61.95	58.93	7.96	36.24

Note: The *BS* determinant or [*D*(*WS'*,*BS'*)-*D*(*WS'*, *BS*)] is obtained by comparing the observed distribution in 2005 and the displaced distribution (g=0.43).

Source: Authors' calculations based on simulated data.

The contribution tends to be higher in the later periods contributing up to almost 40% of the disequalization between 1999 and 2005.[67] Results based on simulated data are surprisingly similar to those based on real data. This means that the procedure can rely on the assumption that log-monthly earnings are well-behaved, and it can therefore be used to isolate the contribution to inequality changes caused by the *BS* determinant.

Now, Table 2.3 shows the contribution of the *BS* determinant to the inequality change using the observed data in the Honduran economy. Appended in this table are the contributions depicted in Table 2.2.

Table 2.3: The macroeconomic (between sectors) earnings-gap effect on labour income inequality changes (Gini Index), observed and simulated data

	Percentage change – Rural distribution		Percentage change – country-level distribution	
Year	Observed gap	Simulated gap	Observed gap	Simulated gap
1991-1999	3.06	-	7.53	-
1999-2005	7.66	7.96	39.11	36.24
2005-2007	-12.38	-	-33.67	-

Source: Authors' calculations based on data from EPHPM I, EPHPM II and random data.

A growing economy incapable to reduce poverty

This paper provides interesting insights to the question why the Honduran economy was incapable to reduce poverty during the first part of the 2000s (see Figure 2.5). The poverty headcount ratio increased more than six percentage points

67 Note that the effects are larger at the country level than in rural areas as the rural income distribution is at the bottom of the overall country distribution and a widening of it has a larger proportionate effect on the overall country distribution.

from 1998 to 2005 while the GDP grew in real terms on average almost 4 percent per year.[68]

The low correlation between poverty reduction and GDP growth can be explained by the inequality dynamics during this period of time. According to Klasen et al. (2012), the Honduran Gini coefficient of the household per-capita income rose from 0.55 to almost 0.61 between 1999 and 2005. The authors argue that the income disequalization during the period 1999-2005 was a rural phenomenon and can be mainly explained by declining labour earnings in the tradable sector (mainly agriculture) and the upsurge of the non-tradable sector.[69]

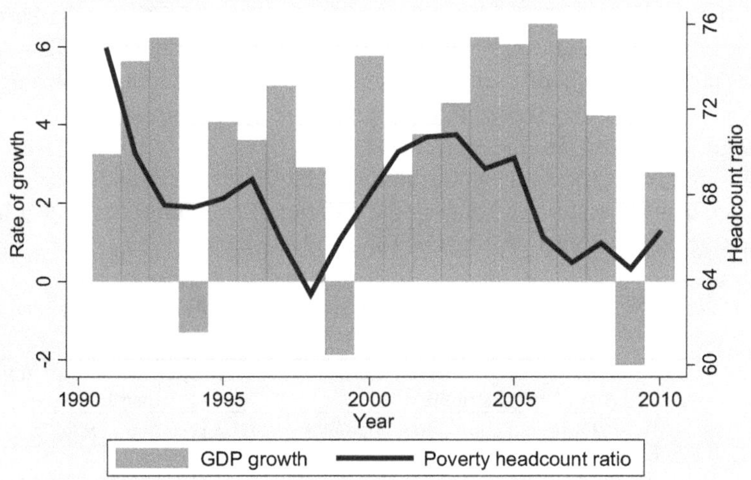

Note: Poverty figures are based on the moderate poverty line (2 US$ per day).
Source: WDI (GDP growth) and UNdata (Poverty).

Figure 2.5: Honduran GDP growth rates and the poverty headcount ratio

Thus, the Honduran path of growth during the early 2000s did not meet the basic pro-poor growth conditions enounced by Klasen (2009) which appear to be very important beyond the specific country context. First, growth did not predominantly take place in neither agriculture nor rural areas where 80% of the poor population actually lives. Secondly, potential workers were not able to diversify into nonfarm sectors or to move to more dynamic regions. Finally, there

68 If we consider only the period 2000-2005, poverty rose by 2 percent while the economy grew on average five percent per year.

69 The divergent trend was more pronounced at the bottom of both distributions.

was not an ex-post pro-poor redistribution of the benefits from growth through the tax and transfer system.

The outcome in terms of poverty during this period of time is not surprising. The poor were seized in rural areas suffering from underemployment or unemployment while earners in other sectors and/or urban areas expanded their labour per-capita incomes over proportionally. Increasing inequality explains why growth does not translate into poverty reduction.

2.6 Conclusions

This paper presents a way to explore how macroeconomic shifts cause inequality changes. It is based on the backwardness observed in the agricultural sector in rural areas. Assuming that an inter-sectoral labour earnings gap exists, this methodology allows to control over the direct impact on inequality changes caused by macroeconomic changes that affect the relative competitiveness between the tradable and non-tradable sectors. The methodology aims to find the labour income gap change (in log units) taking place between two points in time, which is not dependent on the distribution of endowments of the employed population by sectors (observed and unobserved characteristics) and their returns.

First, this paper shows why highly dualistic economies tend to be more unequal than economies with flexible and integrated labour markets. Second, the methodology allows for quantifying the role of direct macroeconomic events on inequality changes. The application here presented shows that almost 40% of the disequalization experienced by the Honduran economy may find their primary cause in macro-conditions (though it does not consider how it affects microeconomic conditions). Klasen et al. (2012) argue that the Mitch Hurricane, declining commodity prices and the appreciation of the RER are the main macroeconomic forces behind the labour income disequalization between 1999 and 2005. Simulated data confirms the results in Klasen et. al. (2012).

The decomposition methodologies support the conclusions by Devillanova et al. (2010) suggesting a channel through which trade integration can affect the labour earnings inequality in a context of capital-skill complementarity and imperfect mobility of workers. The story that follows is that a shift towards the non-tradable sector increases the skill intensity and skill premium in this sector (observed and unobserved ability). This evolution regarding skill intensity and skill premium is backed up by our results regarding the impact of unobservables on inequality in a rural economy characterized by duality. At the same time, relative earnings for less-educated workers also increase in the dynamic sector compared to those in the tradable sector (due to the imperfect mobility). Consequently, skilled and unskilled workers now perform better in the non-tradable sector (relative to those in the tradable sector). In the same manner, the labour income distribution becomes more unequal due to the evolution of the inter-sectoral earnings gap taking place across the whole ability distribution.

Policies oriented towards eliminating the systematic backwardness appear to be highly desirable in such economies. Improvement in the relative competitiveness of the small-scale agricultural activities is consistent with increased rural employment, a reduction in rural underemployment, increasing labour earnings in the tradable sector, a reduction in the earnings gap and consequently, declining inequality levels. As usual, poverty levels are higher in rural areas and amongst those related to agricultural activities. To fight backwardness is thus very similar to reducing poverty and decreasing inequality.

Finally, using fiscal and monetary policy to support the depressed tradable sector appears to be consistent with a rational development strategy in such countries. Among the set of policies that may be used to achieve this goal, it is possible to mention the depreciation of the nominal exchange rate, the attainment of asymmetric trade agreements that recognize the backwardness (fair trade), allowing the imposition of import tariffs and/or export incentives when such backwardness is observed, and the improvement of the rural infrastructure. However, in the long run, it is more important to eliminate the sources of labour immobility across sectors. Immobility forces usually find their explanation in insufficient and outdated educational systems. Therefore, international development assistance should focus principally on improving the coverage and quality of education and infrastructure mainly in rural areas reducing the worker's heterogeneity. Additionally, to guarantee minimum prices for the production of the backward sector may also be considered in such economies, since poverty and inequality are extraordinarily sensitive to the developments in the traditional sector.

Essay 3 - Internal migration and its impact on reducing inter-communal disparities in Chile[iii]

Abstract

Based on the affirmation that internal migration in Chile has become increasingly less important as an equalizing mechanism for regional income disparities, this paper aims to look at the causes of such immobility. The estimation procedure allows for obtaining a non-endogenous potential wage differential which controls for the selectivity process involved in the migration decision (based on observed and unobserved characteristics). This study finds that the productivity differential is the leading factor explaining migration. However, migration not only depends on individual characteristics, but strongly relies on the level of household education. Unfortunately, the initial disadvantages related to adverse family backgrounds determine that the one who faces attractive potential wage differentials is at the same time constrained by its household. The conclusion is that household-related migration costs are a source of inefficiency in labour allocation. Consequently, supporting the infrastructure in the rural economy is not the only way to achieve convergence across the territory. Subsidies aimed to reduce migration costs can be also considered in a framework oriented towards encouraging functional migration flows.

iii This paper was presented at the interdisciplinary conference: "Migration: Global Development, New Frontiers" jointly organized by the NORFACE Research Programme on Migration and the Centre for Research and Analysis of Migration (CReAM) at UCL in 2013, University College London and at the Arnolshain Seminar XI conference by the International Society for Comparative Economic Studies, ISCES, at the University of Antwerp in 2013, Belgium.

3.1 Introduction

Inter-communal migration movements are relatively minor in Chile. From April 2002 to 2006, the Chilean socio-economic household survey (CASEN 2006) reports a flow of 130,197 individuals from communes with less than 40,000 inhabitants to communes with more than 40,000 inhabitants reaching almost 4% of the population at origin.[70] In spite of the dynamic growth experienced in Chile during the past two decades, there is a consensus that the improvement of the standards of living has not been equally distributed across regions or communes. In a context where it is expected that internal migration may work as a mechanism to equalize relative resource scarcities over regions, Soto and Torche (2004) show evidence that migration has become increasingly less important as an equalizing mechanism for regional disparities.[71]

Based on this evidence, this paper focuses on the determinants of inter-communal movements of workers aiming to understand how the selection process of the migrant population works.[72] It considers observed and unobserved characteristics, productivity differentials and initial conditions allowing to asses which factors are currently discouraging migration and thus hampering the equalization of living standards.

In general, individuals are assumed to move if the returns (expected) to migration are greater than the sum of all opportunity costs and the moving costs (Borjas, 1987 and Mincer, 1978). Given this benefit-cost analysis, only a determined group of individuals and households will have an economic incentive to migrate.[73]

There have been many theories trying to explain the migration phenomena at different scales. For instance, the Neoclassical Economic Theory regards migration as a consequence of regional differences on demand and labour supply, which result in wage gaps. Pull factors at destination and push factor at origin

---

70 Individuals moving in the opposite direction reached 128,915; equivalent to 1.1% of the population at origin.

71 Busso (2006) argues, based on evidence by Cuervo González (2003) and Aroca (2004), that migration can also increase regional disparities in Chile.

72 In this paper, rural-urban and urban-rural migration patterns are considered. In 2006, Chile was divided into 13 regions, which are further divided into provinces. Finally, each province is divided into communes. In 2010, Chile consisted of 54 provinces and 346 communes.

73 In this context, positive selection means that, relative to the home-region population, movers are of above-average quality. While common wisdom maintains that movers are the most motivated individuals of the home-region population, it may be possible that persons from the bottom tail of the quality distribution have the economic incentive to migrate.

are the underlying determinants of migration.[74] The micro-economic version considers migration as a result of a rational decision-making process of individuals in which cost-benefit analysis is essential.[75] Todaro (1976) considers that migration is triggered by wage differentials and equilibrium is only reached when the wage differentials tend to be nonexistent. Similarly, Sjaastad (1962) and Becker (1962) propose that migration is an investment decision.

Under the New Economics of Labour Migration (NELM) Theory, migration is a joint decision by household members and not an individual decision (Stark and Bloom, 1985). Following this line of thought, minimizing risk plays a key role in determining migration. In addition, other factors such as capital, credit and insurance market availability also play a role; however, wage differentials are not considered as a necessary condition for migration. The NELM theory considers migration as a household strategy to enhance the income sources. Therefore, remittances play an important role here and migration will thus occur only when the structure and characteristics of the household allow for net gains in welfare.[76]

The Social Network Theory is based on the idea that the flow of information is extremely relevant for potential migrants and their households. It is assumed that family and friends contribute to obtain pertinent information about possible destinations. These networks reduce cost and migration-related risks for newcomers (Tilly and Brown, 1967 and Lomnitz, 1977). Thus, former migrants and non-migrants share information in origin and at destination reducing the risk associated to migration. This is complemented by the theory of cumulative causation, which states that migration reinforces itself by encouraging new migration flows (Massey 1990).

As Tsegai (2007) states, the various theories of migration, though with different policy implications, are not necessarily contradictory to each other. This paper supports the main conclusions of the Neoclassical Economic Theory considering wage differentials as the leading factor explaining migration (triggered by regional differences on demand and labour supply).[77] This paper additionally shows that migration not only depends on individual characteristics, but strongly

74 Well known pull factors at destination are job opportunities, high incomes, amenities, etc. Push factors are usually criminality, poverty, pollution and unemployment amongst others.

75 This micro-economic approach is based on an expected positive net return due to migration (Sjaastad, 1962; Todaro, 1976).

76 Net gains in welfare can be understood, for example, as declining risk and increasing expected incomes.

77 See Borjas (1987), Mincer (1978), Sjaastad (1962), Todaro (1969 and 1976).

relies on household education.[78] Unfortunately, this evidence indicates that it is highly possible that the migrant is not necessarily the one who may benefit from higher wages at the destination (contributing to equalize outputs across regions), but the one who is not constrained by its household. Contrary to this, the one who probably could take advantage from labour market differentials, but belongs to a household with low levels of education, would probably be forced to stay.

This paper also supports the following ideas by the NELM Theory (Stark and Bloom, 1985):

> "It does not view the family as an entity that is split apart as its independence seeking younger members move away in an attempt to dissociate themselves from familial and traditional bondage, regardless of the negative externalities thereby imposed upon their families."
>
> "...this approach shifts the focus of migration theory from individual independence (optimization against nature) to mutual interdependence (optimization against one another), that is, it views migration as a "calculated strategy" and not as an act of desperation or boundless optimism."

The empirical approach of this paper consists of a switching regression model presented by Goldfeld and Quandt (1973) with endogenous switching (Maddala, 1983) which can be properly used as a counterpart from an extended Roy model in the migration context. This methodology contributes through the provision of a structural form for internal migration, which is derived from a powerful theoretical framework. This paper shows that controlling for the selectivity process involved in the migration decision appears to be indispensable. Ignoring the self-selection of the migrant and non-migrant working populations yields to an important underestimation of the potential wage differential. Thus, the estimation of an unbiased potential wage differential for those at origin allows the estimation of a parsimonious structural probability model. This equation has the advantage of accounting for the distribution of unobservables allowing to consistently assess the role of productivity differentials on the migration decision.

The main conclusion is that household matters not only regarding its composition, but also regarding relevant characteristics such as its educational level. The household education captures many underlying migration determinants such as the importance of the loss of income, the access to better information and

---

78 The household education refers to the average education in years, excluding the potential migrant.

networks and their use to reduce migration costs. It might also proxy for the ease of letting go and some demographic components. However, this study is devoted to test the idea that the potential migrant is household-dependent. The mechanisms through which this dependence takes place go beyond the scope of this study.

This study also reveals an interesting conclusion regarding how women (relative to men) are intrinsically motivated to move towards rural communes or remain there (in the case of those already residing in rural communes). At the same time, due to labour market differentials, women are more likely to move towards urban areas or remain there. Such a decomposition of the gender-related effects shows the advantages of using a structural model approach.

Accepting the role of migration costs and amenities in discouraging migration, this paper recognizes that the way to ensure a long-run regional convergence in welfare should be based precisely on lowering migration costs and on the improvement of the rural infrastructure. Such interventions will lead migration to be an effective mechanism in ensuring an efficient allocation of labour between rural and urban communes.

This paper is broken down as follows: Section 3.2 reveals the data and the population of interest. Section 3.3 offers a brief characterization of the migrants and non-migrant groups. The theoretical framework based on the extended Roy model is presented in Section 3.4. Section 3.5 presents the results of the reduced and structural forms for the probability to move as well as the selectivity adjusted wage equations, while Section 3.6 concludes this study.

3.2 The data

For this study, the official data was provided by the *Ministerio de Planificación del Gobierno de Chile* (MIDEPLAN), and in particular the *Encuesta de Caracterización Socioeconómica Nacional 2006* (CASEN 2006) was used.[79] According to MIDEPLAN, the size of CASEN 2006 reaches 73,720 households, with representativeness at country, urban, rural, regional and provincial levels and 301 communes of the country.

This study defines rural communes as those with less than 40,000 inhabitants. For the purpose of robustness, another relevant threshold for this paper was set at 20,000 inhabitants and different specifications regarding the selection of explanatory variables are considered. This paper uses the aforementioned rural-urban definition based on the idea that moving towards another commune

79 Some variables at origin were obtained from CASEN 2003 by MIDEPLAN.

implies a radical lifestyle change, the adoption of housing and job searching decisions, amongst other consequences.

This study is consistent with Coeymans (1983) and Raczynsky (1980). Both studies considered as rural those communes without cities with more than 20,000 inhabitants. The definition in this paper is somewhat different because it instead considers the total communal population. However, the definition adopted in this study considers as urban communes a slightly larger number of communes than those in Coeymans (1983), which is consistent with the urbanization pattern during the last two decades (Pinto da Cunha, 2002). The urban population increased from 85.67% to 87.15% between 2000 and 2006, respectively. Moreover, CASEN 2006 reports that 79% of the population lives within communes of more than 40,000 inhabitants.

This study focuses on the rural-to-urban and urban-to-rural migration patterns. According to this, four categories of individuals can be defined. *Rural* and *Urban Movers* are the individuals who moved within the last four years from rural and urban areas towards urban and rural areas anytime, respectively. *Rural* and *Urban Stayers* are the individuals who remained at origin.

The nature of the data makes it impossible to define a migrant as an individual who has moved to a different commune within the last few years (recent migrant). Consequently, workers who have migrated and later returned to their communes of origin during this period are not considered as migrants. Therefore, the estimates on self-selectivity could be potentially biased towards positive selection regarding the ability distribution. In this study, the population of interest is restricted to non-enrolled workers aged 25 years and older reporting monthly labour earnings in 2006. In order to prevent the endogeneity of the schooling decisions and migration, this study excludes currently enrolled individuals and those who could be enrolled in 2002.

3.3 Ex-post characteristics of inter-communal migrant workers

Table 3.1 shows descriptive information for stayers and movers originating from rural and urban communes.[80] As a matter of fact, movers are younger than and not as experienced as stayers. Rural movers have on average 10.91 years of education, in comparison with the 7.99 years of education for non-migrants origi-

80 The information presented here was collected at destination in 2006. To restrict the sample to those older than 24 years and not being enrolled contributes to approximate the figures to those actually observed at origin (ex-ante).

nating from rural communes. Looking at the average household education, rural movers belong to households with 8.16 years of education per-capita, while the figure for rural stayers reaches only 6.55 years.[81] These figures indicate a positive correlation between education levels and migration from rural to urban communes. Within those originating from rural communes, movers have more children, consist of a slightly larger proportion of women and receive higher monthly earnings than stayers.

Table 3.1: Descriptive statistics for workers in 2006, by groups

	Rural origin		Urban origin	
Variables	Stayers	Movers	Stayers	Movers
Age (in years)	46.52	38.56	44.55	39.56
Potential experience (in years)	32.53	21.66	28.25	22.47
Education (in years)	7.99	10.91	10.31	11.09
Average household education (in years)	6.55	8.16	8.17	8.09
Number of children per household	1.63	1.67	1.73	1.40
Aboriginal origin (*Mapuche*) (%)	9.54	7.64	5.89	6.15
Bi-Parental household (%)	67.42	71.18	67.16	75.14
Female (%)	32.70	34.71	38.73	32.70
Adjusted monthly wage (in Current US$*)	234.60	388.91	380.80	385.04

Note: Based on non-enrolled workers 25 years old and older reporting monthly labour earnings in 2006.
*Average US$ in 2006 equals 524.48 Chilean Pesos.

Source: own elaboration, based CASEN on 2003 CASEN 2006 and Banco Central de Chile.

Regarding those originating from urban communes, the selection of movers seems to be slightly positive in terms of the years of education, but on average, migrants belong to less-educated households. They are also younger, not as experienced, with fewer children and earn slightly more than their non-migrant counterparts.

81 The calculation of the average household education (in years) excludes the potential migrant.

3.4 Theoretical framework

Borjas (1987) used the Roy (1951) model to derive an economic selection model based on unobserved characteristics. In this model, migrants are negatively selected if they have below-average wages and productivities given their observable characteristics. Inversely, positively selected immigrants have above-average earnings and productivities. Thus, there is no relationship between the selection process generated by unobserved characteristics, and the selection process generated by observed characteristics, such as education. In concordance with the kernel of the Harris-Todaro (1970) model, well-educated individuals are more able to access good-quality information on the labour market in potential destinations and therefore, highly educated people are more likely to get a job than unskilled workers if the correlation between labour markets in both regions is strong enough. However, as Borjas (1988) states:

> "It is completely possible for the most educated persons to migrate to the U.S. (i.e. positive selection in education), but for these persons to be the least productive persons in the population of highly educated persons (i.e. negative selection in unobserved characteristics)."

There are consequently two dimensions of "quality", therefore, generalizations based only on observed characteristics are misleading, because much more than half of the variance in wage rates or weekly earnings is explained by unobserved characteristics.

The standard Roy model predicts that migrants will be negatively selected if the inequality in the distribution of incomes is lower at destination than at origin and if the correlation between wages in both regions is strong enough. Nevertheless, a generalization of the Roy model that relaxes the assumption of constant moving costs by allowing correlation between non-observed abilities and moving costs shows that the type of selection may change in either direction (Borjas, 1987).[82]

---

82 The standard Roy model does not consider any switching costs. As a consequence of this, important information is not taken into account if the costs of moving are inversely related to the amounts of human capital. If this is the case, it is plausible that individuals on the top of the income distribution at home (origin) decide to move to a host area with a more equal wage distribution (positive selection). One of the conclusions of this study shows that, in fact, the costs of moving are inversely related to the amount of human capital.

3.4.1 Extended Roy model

This model, presented by Borjas (1988), considers random mobility costs. The log wages at home area are described by:

$$lnW_1 = u_1 + e_1 \qquad (1)$$

Where u_1 is the average log wage at the home area and e_1 is the zero mean disturbance with variance σ_1^2. In the same way, the log wages at host area are defined such that:

$$lnW_2 = u_2 + e_2 \qquad (2)$$

Both wage distributions have a joint normal distribution, where e_1 and e_2 can be interpreted as unobservable abilities of individuals.

Assuming that C represents the migration costs which, in this extension of the standard Roy model, are not fixed but rather a proportion of the monetary and non-monetary cost of migration as a proportion of home income. Migration occurs if:[83]

$$\frac{W_2 - W_1}{W_1} > C$$

The extended version of the standard Roy model assumes that $C = \gamma + \varepsilon$ (3) is normally distributed with mean γ and error $\varepsilon \sim N(0, \sigma_\varepsilon^2)$. With this information, an individual moves if the index function $I^* = (u_2 - u_1 - \gamma + e_2 - e_1 - \varepsilon) > 0$ and stays if $I^* \leq 0$. Assuming the normality conditions and defining:

$$\sigma^v = \sqrt{Var(e_2 - e_1 - \varepsilon)}, \quad z = -\frac{u_2 - u_1 - \gamma}{\sigma^v} \text{ and } \eta = \frac{e_2 - e_1 - \varepsilon}{\sigma^v}$$

The probability to move is given by:

$$Pr(\eta > z) = 1 - \Phi(z) \qquad (4)$$

Where $\Phi()$ is the cumulative distribution of the standard normal and following Heckman (1979), the unobserved wage of a mover in the region of origin is given by:

83 This inequality approximates $lnW_2 - lnW_1 > C$.

$$E(lnW_1|I^* > 0) = u_1 + \frac{\sigma_1\sigma_2}{\sigma^\nu}\left[(\rho_{1,2} - \frac{\sigma_1}{\sigma_2}) - \rho_{1,\varepsilon}\frac{\sigma_\varepsilon}{\sigma_2}\right]\lambda \quad (5)$$

and the observed wages at destination as:

$$E(lnW_2|I^* > 0) = u_2 + \frac{\sigma_1\sigma_2}{\sigma^\nu}\left[(\frac{\sigma_2}{\sigma_1} - \rho_{1,2}) - \rho_{2,\varepsilon}\frac{\sigma_\varepsilon}{\sigma_1}\right]\lambda \quad (6)$$

Where $\rho_{1,2}$ represents the correlation coefficient between the disturbances e_1 and e_2. $\rho_{1,\varepsilon}$ and $\rho_{2,\varepsilon}$ are the correlation coefficients between e_1 and the error of the moving cost ε and between e_2 and ε respectively.
$\lambda(z) = \frac{\phi(z)}{1-\Phi(z)}$ is the inverse of Mill´s ratio where $\phi()$ is the standard normal density function.

Brücker and Trübswetter (2007) decompose the second terms in (5) and (6) in order to identify composition and scale effects.[84] It reveals important implications about the selection biases in terms of unobserved and observed characteristics. Borjas (1988) shows that positive selection in observed characteristics (i.e. schooling) occurs if the labour market in the host region offers a higher return in comparison to the home region. The estimation strategy presented in the next section achieves the assessment of a structural probability model for internal migration, controlling for observed characteristics as well as for the impact of unobservables.

3.4.2 Estimation

The extended Roy model presented in this paper finds a suitable counterpart in a switching regression model presented by Goldfeld and Quandt (1973) with endogenous switching (Maddala and Nelson, 1975; Maddala, 1983).[85]

$$I_i = \delta(lnW_{2i} - lnW_{1i}) - Z_i\psi - \varepsilon_i \quad (7)$$

Where equation (1) and (2) can be rewritten as:

84 The composition effect measures how a change in the ability mix of a constant-sized immigrant pool affects the selection bias, holding the size of the flow constant. The scale effect captures what happens to the selection bias as the size of the flow is increased for any given mix of abilities.

85 Endogenous switching satisfies that $(\mu_{1i}, \mu_{2i}, \varepsilon_i) \sim N(0, \Sigma)$, where $\Sigma = \begin{bmatrix} \sigma_{11} & \sigma_{12} & \sigma_{1\varepsilon} \\ \sigma_{12} & \sigma_{22} & \sigma_{2\varepsilon} \\ \sigma_{1\varepsilon} & \sigma_{2\varepsilon} & 1 \end{bmatrix}$ is the covariance Matrix.

$$lnW_{1i} = X_{1i}\beta_1 + \mu_{1i} \quad (8)$$

$$lnW_{2i} = X_{2i}\beta_2 + \mu_{2i} \quad (9)$$

Here, X_1 is a vector of personal and household characteristics determining wages. As standard in the literature, it contains educational levels and the potential experience (and its square). It additionally includes the average years of education for the other household members. Controls for those belonging to the *Mapuche* ethnic group, gender, wealthy communes, rural areas, occupations, economic sectors, the public sector and dummies for the region of residence (at destination) are also considered.

However, the index function cannot be estimated in a structural form because $lnW_{2i} - lnW_{1i}$ is endogenous. To solve this endogeneity problem, Lee (1978) and Willis and Rosen (1979) propose a three step strategy.

In the first step, a reduced form of the migration index function is estimated by using a probit Maximum Likelihood estimator where $I_i = 1$ if $I^* > 0$ and $I_i = 0$ otherwise. This index function is based on the migration cost identity $Z_i\psi + \varepsilon_i = C$ (counterpart of (3)), which depends on personal and household characteristics in Z_i and unobservable ε_i.

Vector Z_i consists of the level of education of the potential migrant. Here, a positive association is expected owing to the relevance of education in the migration decision. Education allows individuals to reduce risk and improves their employment probabilities abroad.[86]

Following Stark and Bloom (1985), the degree in which the remaining members of the household can generate income is important information for the potential migrant. So this paper includes the average household education (excluding the potential migrant) in the model. Other variables usually considered in the literature and included in this study are: the potential experience and its square, gender, the number of children in the household, a control indicating bi-parental households, indigenous status (as above), and controls for the regions at origin. All these variables are expected to be proxies of the characteristics of interest at origin (ex-ante). Additionally, the communal unemployment rates at origin are included to reflect the held notion that unemployment (and the subsequent poverty and lack of opportunities) encourages migration. The log-population at origin aims to control for the availability of public goods, as two indicators accounting for changes in the relative communal connectivity are ex-

86 Greenwood (1975) argues also that education may reduce the psychological costs of migration.

pected to control the fact that migration flows are not homogeneously distributed across the territory. The inclusion of interaction terms between these indexes and the household education are expected to additionally show the relevance of the human capital accumulation within the household in shaping the observed migration patterns (see below).

In a second step, the ML function uses the estimated parameters from the reduced form probit model as starting values for the estimation of the Heckman corrected wage equations.[87] In order to identify this system, at least one variable in Z_i must be not included in X_1.[88]

$$I_i^* = \delta(X_{2i}\beta_2 - X_{1i}\beta_1) + \delta(\mu_{2i} - \mu_{1i}) - \varepsilon_i = Z_i^*\psi^* + \varepsilon_i^* \qquad (10)$$

Now, the parameter vector $\hat{\psi}^*$ in (10) can be suitably estimated and therefore, the inverse Mills' ratio for stayers and migrants can be calculated. Equations (11) and (12) can be estimated for each worker, so that the potential differential wage can be calculated. For stayers:

$$lnW_i = X_i\beta_1 - \sigma_{e_{1\eta}} \frac{\phi(Z_i^*\hat{\psi}^*)}{\Phi(Z_i^*\hat{\psi}^*)} + \mu_{1i} \qquad (11)$$

And for movers:

$$lnW_i = X_i\beta_2 - \sigma_{e_{2\eta}} \frac{\phi(Z_i^*\hat{\psi}^*)}{1-\Phi(Z_i^*\hat{\psi}^*)} + \mu_{2i} \qquad (12)$$

Both wage equations (for stayers and movers) allow the estimation of a potential wage differential for each worker without selection bias. The potential wage differential (in logs) and its square (allowing for nonlinearities) are then included in the third step to estimate structurally the index function for the migration probability (10). Besides the potential wage differential, the structural equation includes as explanatory variables the communal unemployment rates at

---

87 This paper uses the Heckman Maximum Likelihood estimator for survey data, which also takes into account the correlation between primary sample units avoiding the underestimation of standard errors and, consequently, avoiding the overestimation of sample selection bias or possible self-selectivity of migrants. The maximum likelihood method has been shown to produce consistent estimates under a few plausible conditions. Maximum likelihood estimates have the further advantage of being normal and efficient if sample sizes are large enough (Gujarati, 2003: p.113).

88 This identification problem was solved using the marital status and the indexes of changes in connectivity as exclusion variables in (11) and (12) to identify (10).

origin and the provision of public goods proxied by the population at origin (in logs). Additionally, in order to control for the life cycle of the potential migrant, the age is included.[89] In order to test the hypothesis that migration is a household-dependent decision which is also affected by channels unrelated to the labour market, the average household education is included in the structural model specifications. Finally, other relevant characteristics are also considered i.e. the bi-parental household condition, the number of children in the household, indigenous status (*Mapuche*) dummies for the regions of origin, interaction terms and connectivity indices as well.

3.4.3 The role of geographic connectivity - Adjacency at the communal level

This paper uses a social network method to understand the role of the "*connectivity*" in determining migration. The migration literature has extensively depicted the role of the distance affecting the decision to migrate (Greenwood, 1995).[90] However, distance itself is not a migration determinant, but it can be seen as an inverse function of the connection between origin and destination. Consequently, how connected are communes at origin and destination can be considered as a proper proxy for underlying migration determinants such as information flows, transport cost, psychological and opportunity costs (Schwartz, 1973 and Greenwood, 1995). To capture the impact of changes in connectivity, an index is elaborated following Boots and Kanaroglou (1988). The index relies on the principal eigenvector of the connectivity matrix.[91] Each element of the principal eigenvector *e* is a measure of the location relative to the "*centre*".

Due to the peculiar geographical distribution of the Chilean communes, two connectivity index variables are needed. $Comm_{ij}$ is expected to control for changes in the relative connectivity at the regional level and R_{ab} at the country level based on migration flows between regions. These variables can complement the evidence found decades ago by Herrick (1965) and Elizaga (1970) showing that migration in Chile follows a "stair-shaped" process, where individuals migrate initially from small towns towards intermediate cities and thereafter towards metropolitan areas.

89 Following Greenwood (1993) the migration propensity decreases with age.

90 See also Beaudreau (1990).

91 This squared matrix is also known as the adjacency matrix. In this matrix, adjacent communes (regions) are denoted by the unity, while the diagonal of the matrix and non-adjacent communes (regions) have only zeros.

The index of the relative location change between communes is obtained as follows:

$$Comm_{ij,ab} = \left[\frac{e_{j,b}-e_{i,a}}{e_{j,b}+e_{i,a}}\right] \tag{13}$$

Where *e* represents the elements of the principal eigenvector of the connectivity matrix and subscripts *i* and *a* denote the commune and region of origin respectively. In the same way, subscripts *j* and *b* represent the commune and region of destination. Communes *j* and *i* may or may not belong to the same region. In the same way:

$$R_{ab} = \left[\frac{e_b-e_a}{e_b+e_a}\right] \tag{14}$$

Both indices take values between -1 and 1 including the zero, which mean no change in the relative location by region and/or commune. Therefore, using a single multiplicative index is unsuitable. Values close to 1 indicate a location change from an extreme peripheral commune (region) towards a central commune (region). Values close to -1 indicate the opposite.

Figure 3.1 shows the distribution of the mentioned indexes described above. Regarding migration flows between different regions R_{ab}, migrants tend to move towards relatively more peripheral regions. An unconditional view of the data shows that, except for *Puente Alto* (Región Metropolitana), the most preferred destinations for inter-regional migrants are placed in relatively non-central regions such as: IV (*La Serena*), IX (*Temuco*), II (*Antofagasta*) and I (*Iquique*). When considering inter-communal migration at a regional level, the opposite occurs. Migrants move more frequently from peripheral communes towards those with a higher connectivity index. Note that in this study, the impact of changes in the index of connectivity is predetermined by the migration pattern. However, this control is needed in order to obtain consistent estimates of the other determinants of migration. Additionally, interaction terms relating the household education to the connectivity indexes are also considered (*Interaction 1* = average household education × $Comm_{ij}$ and *Interaction 2* = average household education × R_{ab}). The interaction terms aim to test whether the decision to move towards a more connected/unconnected region or commune depends on the household education. It is expected to find a significant coefficient for these interactions, at least for those coming from rural areas. This would be an indication that migration flows consist, in a major part, of those who belong to households with relatively high levels of education. The evidence in CASEN 2006 is quite clear regarding this issue. Two-thirds of the migrant population comes from relatively well-educated households (above average).[92]

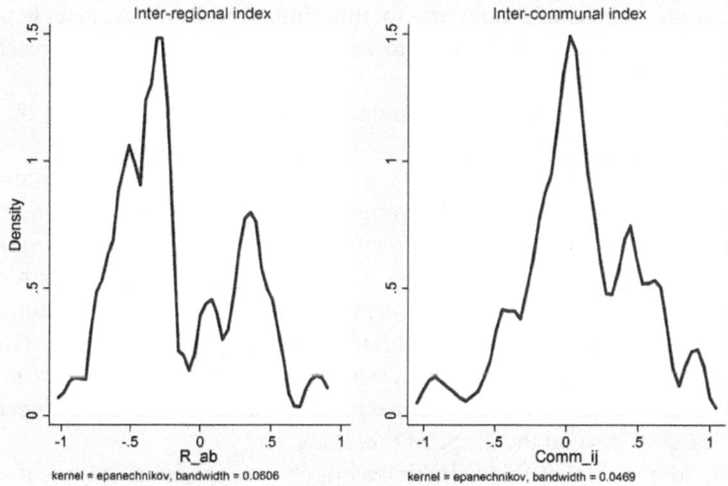

Source: Authors' calculations based on self-generated connectivity matrices.

Figure 3.1: Distribution of the connectivity change indexes (all flows, 2002-2006)

3.4.4 Household education

As Stark and Bloom (1985) state, the degree to which the remaining members of the household can generate income is important information for the potential migrant. It is not risky to believe that the household income generation capacity is correlated with the stock of education in the household.[93] Thus, less-educated households are more dependent on the monetary and non-monetary contribution of each member. The cost in case of migration will be somewhat proportional to the household welfare dependence on any household member and therefore, an individual would be able to move, given other conditions, if he or she knows that in the case of migration the household will not suffer a considerable reduction in welfare.

92 See also Table 3.1.

93 This variable was generated excluding the years of education of the potential migrant. More important than to avoid the endogeneity problems, it is possible to figure out what the potential migrant is observing in its own household in terms of education.

This variable is also highly correlated with the dependency ratio, but conditional on the stock of education within the household. Poor levels of household education would reflect high levels of dependency, which translate into high opportunity costs in the form of higher reservation wages for potential migration (discouraging migration). Contrary to this, high levels of average household education would be associated with lower dependency ratios, lower reservation wages and better mobility prospects.

In summary, the household education captures many underlying migration determinants such as the importance of the loss of income (opportunity costs in terms of household income at origin), but also the access to better information and networks and their use to reduce migration costs. It might represent the ease of letting go (more educated parents may find it easier to let their children leave the household) and some demographic components (younger siblings will typically have higher educational levels than their parents). This paper aims to assess whether the theoretical reasons briefly depicted above find some empirical support and can easily help to characterize the initial constraints that potential migrants might face. However, the mechanism through which this dependence takes place goes beyond the scope of this study.

It would appear that this variable has rarely been used in empirical studies. For instance, and for a variety of micro and macro model specifications to test for self-selection of migrants, Yashiv (2004), Brücker and Jahn (2008), Cobb-Clark (1993), Cohen and Haberfeld (2007), Brücker and Defoort (2007), Parrado and Cerrutti (2003) and Abramitzky (2009) used only individual education variables in their models. Fafchamps and Shilpi (2008) additionally use the father's education level in the migration selection equation. Tsegai (2007) uses the average years of education of the adult household members and finds a probit-coefficient for average education years for adults in the household equals 0.126 at the 1% significance level in the probability model of the migration decision equation at the household level in the Volta Basin of Ghana.

3.5 Estimation results

As mentioned earlier, the three-step strategy aims to obtain consistent estimates of the individual probability to migrate. In the first step, the probit model for migration serves as the starting point for the estimation of a wage equation allowing to independently evaluate wage determinants for migrants and stayers accounting for the role of unobservables and their self-selection (second step). Finally, in the third step, the structural probability model explores, amongst other determinants, the role of the non-endogenous potential wage differential and the average household education in the migration probability.

3.5.1 Probit - reduced form (first step)

Rural-urban migration

Table 3.2 shows the reduced forms of the migration probability models.[94] The probit estimates indicate a positive relationship between education and the probability to move. This effect is stronger for individuals with higher levels of education. Bi-parental households are significantly associated with higher probability to migrate. The number of children per household does not have any significant impact on the probability to move. As expected, average household education positively affects the probability to move, while having an indigenous background does not affect the probability to move.

The potential experience discourages the migration. As expected, higher communal unemployment rate at origin increases the migration probability towards urban areas. The statistical significance of the connectivity change indices shows that the geographical network structure should be taken into account in a conditional framework. At the regional level, the net migration flow goes from the centre towards communes placed in the periphery. However, many important cities are located in peripheral areas within a region. At the country level, the net migration flow originating from rural communes goes from "isolated" regions towards regions in the "*centre*".[95] Finally, the significant coefficient on the log-population variable indicates that the provision of public goods works as a pull factor discouraging migration. Interaction terms appear to be insignificant.

Urban-rural migration

Here, the probability of migrating is statistically significantly dependent on the level of education. The idea that education allows individuals to reduce risks, improving their employment probabilities abroad appears to be confirmed.

---

94 Table C.1 in Appendix shows the same models using the alternative threshold (set at 20,000 inhabitants).

95 This finding cannot be interpreted as contrary to the conclusions by Herrick (1965) and Elizaga (1970).

Education encourages migration independently of the flow direction. As expected (due to the nature of the flow), the index of relative connectivity change indicate that migration flows towards regions in the periphery.[96]

Table 3.2: Reduced form of the index function, probit ML. Threshold set at 40,000 inhabitants, 2002-2006 (first step)

Dependent variable: migrant status

	Rural-Urban			Urban-Rural		
Variables \ Model	M1	M2	M3	M1	M2	M3
Basic education	0.35***	0.23**	0.21**	-0.0122	0.069*	0.069*
Secondary education	0.60***	0.39***	0.33***	-0.0386	0.098**	0.098**
Tertiary education	0.72***	0.38**	0.34**	-0.0488	0.17***	0.17***
Potential experience >5 <11	-0.328	-0.247	-0.199	0.021	-0.0283	-0.0282
Potential experience >10 <16	-0.58**	-0.497*	-0.44*	-0.064	-0.138*	-0.138*
Potential experience >15	-0.89***	-0.86***	-0.84***	-0.39***	-0.42***	-0.42***
Avg. household education	-	0.05***	0.06***	-	-0.03***	-0.03***
$Comm_{ij}$	-2.8***	-2.8***	-4.7***	-	-	-
R_{ab}	1.97***	1.93***	0.745	-3.00***	-2.99***	-3.05***
Interaction 1	-	-	0.21	-	-	-
Interaction 2	-	-	0.139	-	-	0.008
Bi-parental household	0.27***	0.30***	0.32***	0.24***	0.22***	0.22***
Number of Children	-0.01	0.017	0.028	-0.10***	-0.12***	-0.12***
Mapuche	-0.072	-0.059	-0.06	-0.035	-0.054	-0.054
Female	0.027	0.03	0.037	-0.09**	-0.09***	-0.09***
Unemp. rates at origin	0.09***	0.09***	0.09***	-0.04***	-0.045***	-0.045***
Log of population at origin	-0.172**	-0.19**	-0.19**	0.031	0.039	0.039
Constant	-0.58	-0.76	-0.93	-2.2***	-2.01***	-2.01***
Regional controls		Yes			Yes	
Observations		51278			47452	
Non-migrant Population		1006382			3990350	
Migrant Population		41501			47592	
Population Size		1047883			4037942	
F	12.04	12.11	11.56	20.76	23.34	22.49
Prob > F	0.0000	0.0000	0.0000	0.0000	0.0000	0.0000

Significance levels: *** p<0.01, ** p<0.05, * p<0.1.

Note: Based on non-enrolled workers 25 years old and older reporting monthly labour wages in 2006.

Source: Own calculations based on CASEN 2003 and CASEN 2006.

The number of children and the labour experience are significantly associated to lower probabilities of moving. Finally, women are less likely to mi-

96 The coefficient of the index at the communal level could not be calculated due to the insufficient number of observations with positive output.

grate, while the indigenous background appears to be uncorrelated with the probability to move.

3.5.2 Selectivity adjusted wage equations and the potential wage differential

Accounting for the selection process involved in the migration decision, Table 3.3 shows the monthly wage equations for movers and non-migrant workers (threshold set at 40,000 inhabitants).[97] Although unbiased wage estimates are needed to consistently obtain the migration probabilities, they also deserve attention. With independence of the threshold being used, wage equations for movers and stayers show the expected influence of the standard determinants on wages.[98] However, some interesting results can be found in these equations. For example, consistent with the fact that women are relatively over-represented in the sample of rural movers and under-represented in the sample of urban movers (relative to their stayer counterparts, see Table 3.1), women's earnings appear to be "less-penalized" for movers than for stayers originating from rural communes. Contrary to this, women originating from urban communes are expected to earn less in the case of migration. It is important to keep in mind that women movers perform differently than their stayer counterparts. This can help to explain the findings in the structural model.[99]

The same tables show that returns to education are higher for movers than for stayers. This finding points out that the observed positive selection in education is related to the observed outputs in the labour markets. However, the earning distribution is not only dependent on the relative returns to education and its distribution, but also on the distribution of unobservables and its returns. For movers originating in rural areas the results indicate that, in terms of unobserved ability, they can be considered a random sample of the population at origin.

Contrary to this, for stayers originating from rural communes, the inverse Mill's ratio λ turns out to have a significant and positive impact on wages. This indicates that the self-selection process involves only those who decide to stay at origin. Equations (11) and (12) show that the total impact of self-selection on expected incomes can be calculated by the difference between the coefficients associated to inverse Mill's ratio for movers and stayers.

97 Table C.2 in Appendix shows the wage equations using the alternative threshold set at 20,000 inhabitants.

98 For robustness purposes, we estimate the adjusted wage equations using the best reduced form model (M2) and the alternative threshold set at 20,000 inhabitants.

99 The structural effect of being a woman on migration excludes the consequences of being a woman working through the labour market (affecting the wages at origin and destination).

On average, the effect of self-selection on expected incomes is about 36% and 4% for those originating from rural and urban communes, respectively. Therefore, ignoring this issue would strongly underestimate the potential wage differential for those originating from rural communes.

Table 3.3: Wage equations adjusted for self-selection. Movers and stayers. Threshold set at 40,000 inhabitants using M2 (second step)

Dependent variable: monthly wages (threshold set at 40,000 inhabitants)

	Rural Origin		Urban Origin	
Variables / Migrant status	Movers	Stayers	Movers	Stayers
Basic education	0.164	0.107***	0.168**	0.135***
Secondary education	0.208	0.294***	0.380***	0.317***
Tertiary education	0.853***	0.637***	0.756***	0.685***
Potential experience >5 <11	0.788***	0.175***	0.0811	0.219***
Potential experience >10 <16	0.626**	0.310***	0.194	0.355***
Potential experience >15	0.757***	0.383***	0.197	0.425***
Average household education	0.00442	0.0364***	0.0501***	0.0364***
Number of children in household	-0.00859	0.0269***	0.0759***	0.0360***
Mapuche	-0.122	0.0226	0.0421	-0.022
Female	-0.342***	-0.500***	-0.552***	-0.415***
Public sector	0.023	0.0532***	0.0147	-0.0275
Rich commune	0.543***	-	0.0724	0.263***
Rural sector	-0.00436	0.0923***	0.0321	-0.124***
Inverse Mill's ratio (*Lambda*)	-0.0767	0.292***	0.0102	0.0499
Constant	9.105***	9.105***	9.276***	9.276***
Occupational controls	Yes	Yes	Yes	Yes
Sectoral controls	Yes	Yes	Yes	Yes
Regional controls	Yes	Yes	Yes	Yes
Observations	51278	51278	32234	32234
Population size	1047883	1047883	4037942	4037942
Censored population	1006382	41501	3990350	47592
F	155.9	401.6	29.73	242.2
Prob > F	0.0000	0.0000	0.0000	0.0000

Significance levels: *** p<0.01, ** p<0.05, * p<0.1.

Note: Based on non-enrolled workers 25 years old and older reporting monthly labour wages in 2006.

Source: Own calculations based on CASEN 2003 and CASEN 2006.

The potential wage differential and education

Now, after controlling for the selectivity of the migration decision (to stay or to move), it is possible to analyze the relationship between the potential wage differential conditional on the education of the potential migrant and on the average education of its household. Figure 3.2 shows the distribution of the potential wage differential for the bottom and upper tails of the educational distribution. The left panel shows that a significant portion of those with tertiary education "*observe*" a potential wage differential larger than 0.5 log-points.

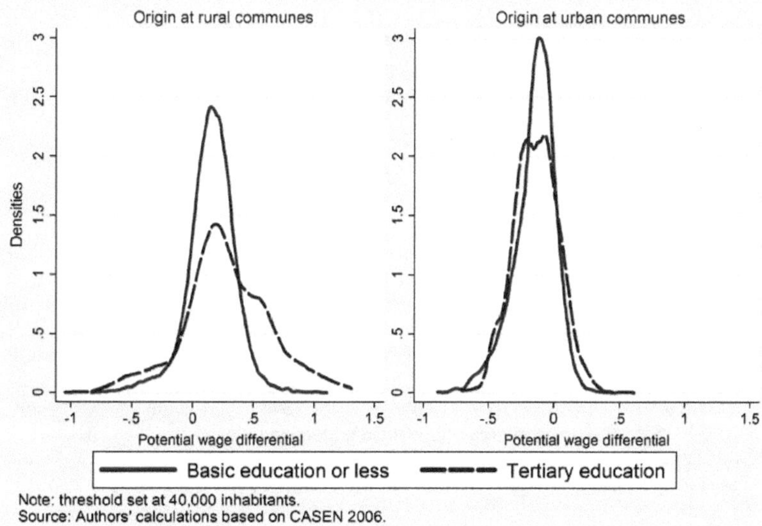

Figure 3.2: Distribution potential wage differential, tertiary versus basic education or less (threshold: 40,000 inhabitants, 2002-2006)

Following the idea that migration is an investment decision (Becker, 1962 and Sjaastad, 1962), migration is more likely to occur when the potential wage differential overcomes all moving costs. Table 3.4 shows that migration is not a rare event for workers at origin facing potential wage differentials larger than 0.5 log-points (mostly tertiary educated). Contrary to this, migration is significantly less frequent for those with potential wage gaps smaller than 0.5 log-points.

Turning the relationship between the average household education and the potential wage differential, Figure 3.3 shows that for those originating from rural areas, lower levels of household education are associated with large productivity differentials.

On average, only those belonging to households with about 10 years of education or less actually observe positive potential wage gaps. This finding is crucial in the interpretation of the structural probability model.

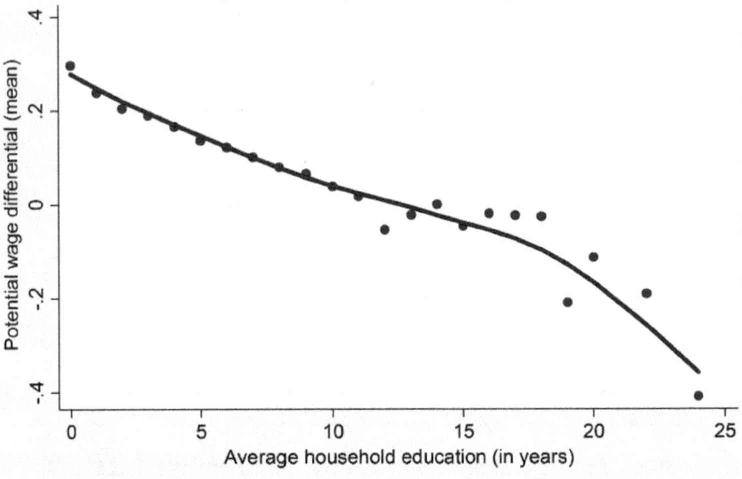

Figure 3.3: The potential wage differential and the average household education (threshold: 40,000 inhabitants, 2002-2006)

Table 3.4: Migration incidence by groups

	Wage gap < 0.5 log points		Wage gap > 0.5 log points	
Migration status	Frequency	Percentage	Frequency	Percentage
Movers	29,015	2.69	12,486	17.94
Stayers	1,050,752	97.31	57,103	82.06

Source: Authors' calculations based on CASEN 2006.

3.5.3 Probit, structural form (third step)

Table 3.5 confirms that there is a significant causal relationship between the potential wage differential and the migration decision.[100] This relationship is depicted in Figure 3.4. Interestingly, when the potential wage differential is

100 Table C.3 in the Appendix shows the results of the structural form using the alternative threshold set at 20,000 inhabitants.

smaller than a certain threshold, the probability to move is almost independent to small changes in the potential wage differential. However, beyond the threshold, the migration probability increases exponentially.[101]

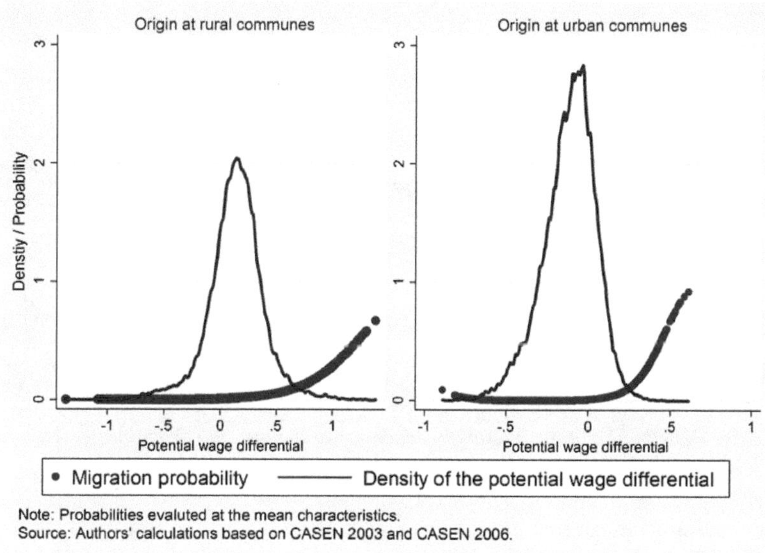

Figure 3.4: Potential wage differential and migration probabilities (at the mean characteristics, 2002-2006)

Household education

The average household education appears to be highly significant in all specifications for reduced and structural forms of the probability models. Figure 3.5 shows for a worker with average characteristics originating from a rural commune, how the migration probability grows with additional years of household education. The relevance of the household education on migration can be driven from an example based on the results of the structural probability model.

---

101 The mentioned threshold can be understood as the cost term in an indirect utility function, and consequently, the bigger the threshold, the higher the migration costs.

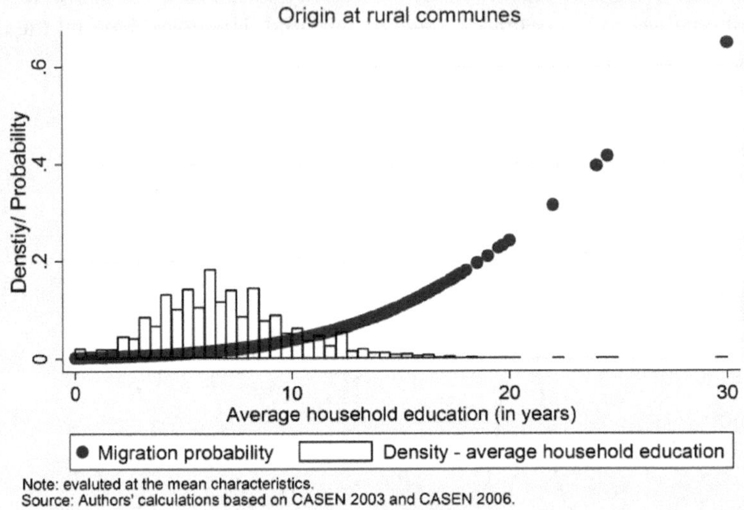

Figure 3.5: Distribution of the household education and migration probabilities from rural to urban communes (at mean characteristics, 2002-2006)

According to these results, the "average" worker originating from rural areas has 8 years of education (being non-tertiary educated), 6.6 years of household education and faces a potential wage differential of 0.125 log-points. Looking at the figure 3.4, it is possible to realize that this average worker has an extremely low probability of moving. Now, imagine that the same worker belongs to a household with an average of 20 or 25 years of education. In this case, this worker would have a migration probability of about 24% and 43%, respectively (extraordinarily high in the context of migration).

This example points out that migration is not an individual decision, and that it depends largely on the household education. Moreover, the structural probability model allows to decompose the impact of the household education into labour and non-labour market effects. The effect working through the labour market discourages migration.

Potential migrants belonging to well-educated household face lower productivity differentials than those having families with low levels of human capital and they are therefore less likely to migrate.

Table 3.5: Structural form of the index function, probit ML, 2002-2006. Threshold set at 40,000 inhabitants using M2 (third step)

Dependent variable: migration status.

	Rural-Urban			Urban-Rural		
Variables	M1	M2	M3	M1	M2	M3
Log-wage differential	0.76***	1.21***	1.28***	3.16***	3.56***	3.59***
Log-wage diff. (squared)	1.15***	0.69***	0.624**	4.84***	4.89***	4.89***
Age	-0.02***	-0.02***	-0.02***	-0.01***	-0.01***	-0.008***
Avg. household educ.	-	0.107***	0.10***	-	-0.05***	-0.05***
$Comm_{ij}$	-2.63***	-2.62***	-	-	-	-
R_{ab}	2.15***	2.03***	-	-2.92***	-2.89***	-2.91***
Interaction 1	-	-	-0.22***	-	-	-
Interaction 2	-	-	0.24***	-	-	0.0032
Bi-parental household	0.28***	0.332***	0.34***	0.334***	0.304***	0.304***
Number of children	-0.021	0.0386	0.044	-0.223***	-0.28***	-0.275***
Mapuche	-0.029	0.099	0.092	-0.209***	-0.29***	-0.298***
Female	-0.123*	-0.20***	-0.20***	0.230***	0.301***	0.301***
Unemp. rates at origin	0.089***	0.088***	0.09***	-0.06***	-0.06***	-0.061***
Log of pop. at origin	-0.16**	-0.234***	-0.23***	0.06*	0.09***	0.09***
Constant	-0.319	-0.664	-0.69	-2.24***	-2.12***	-2.12***
Regional controls		Yes			Yes	
Observations		51,278			47,452	
Non-migrant Population		1,006,382			3,990,350	
Migrant Population		41,501			47,592	
Population Size		1,047,883			4,037,942	
F	15.7	16.16	17.98	43.2	40.94	39.28
Prob > F	0.00	0.00	0.00	0.00	0.00	0.00

Significance levels: *** p<0.01, ** p<0.05, * p<0.1.

Note: Based on non-enrolled workers 25 years old and older reporting monthly labour earnings in 2006.

Source: Own calculations based on CASEN 2003 and CASEN 2006.

Contrary to this, the structural impact, which is not related to the labour market, encourages migration.[102] As a result, the one who could take advantage from a labour market differential, but belongs to the segment of less-educated households will probably be forced to stay.

The correlation between the potential wage differential and the household education is statistically significant for all patterns and all specifications in this study. Thus, to ignore the household education yields biased estimates of the productivity differentials on migration probability.[103]

102 Such decomposition arises by comparing structural and reduced form estimates.

103 As a consequence of this, the role of education on the migration probability is overestimated in reduced form equations.

Thus, household-level migration costs are a source of inefficiency when labour markets allocate workers between rural and urban communes.

Regarding the urban-rural pattern of migration, the household education reduces the migration probability. However, the impact is small and can be interpreted as a pull factor resulting from larger returns of this variable in more populated areas. As migration here is not positively dependent on the household education and the distribution of the potential wage differential is similar across educational levels (right panel in Figure 3.2), it can be argued that potential movers are not being constrained by their initial conditions and therefore, migration is probably working efficiently at least in the urban rural migration pattern.

The gender issue

Looking at our results, it is possible to draw some conclusions based on a gender perspective. The structural model shows that there are two channels in which being a woman affects the migration probability. The first one is related to the labour markets, in particular, to the potential wage differential which captures the fact that women movers are "less penalized" in terms of monthly earnings than their stayer counterparts as they originate from rural areas (Table 3.3). The second channel is related to the women's preferences which are non-related to the labour markets. As a result, reduced form estimates show the (confounded) combined effect of these two forces working in opposite directions. Thus, the gender issue is not irrelevant in designing and implementing migration-related policies.

The same reasoning follows for those originating from urban areas. The structural form actually shows that females are more likely to migrate than males towards rural communes. However, because women are worst-off regarding earnings in case of migration (and this discourages migration relative to males), the aggregate effect is significantly negative. Thus, women (relative to men) are intrinsically motivated to move/stay towards (or stay in) rural communes while labour market differentials push and pull women towards urban areas.

Other determinants

To be part of a bi-parental household increases the migration probability. This result should be carefully interpreted because it might reflect the notion that migration can be a sequential process. Therefore, this variable eventually contains information related to migration experience and is consequently not only capturing the restriction imposed by the structure of the household. The number of children per household appears to be not correlated with the migration probability for those originating from rural communes. However, for those with origin in urban areas, the decomposition of the effect indicates that children appear to increase the potential wage differential (this is based on the idea that workers with children behave differently than those without children in terms of productivity). Contrary to this and as expected, the direct impact of the number of children in the household discourages migration.

Regarding the ethnic background (*Mapuche*), the structural model helps to disentangle its impact for those originating from urban areas. Here, labour markets appear to push those with indigenous background towards rural areas, while other factors non-related to the labour market appear to work in the opposite direction. Hence, the global impact appears to be insignificant (showed in the reduced form). For those originating in rural areas, the ethnic background does not play any significant role. Regarding the life cycle variable (age), this shows as expected a negative association with the studied probability. Looking at the interaction terms, they are only significant towards urban areas keeping the direction of the original indexes. This means a significant relationship between the connectivity change and the household education. Thus the migration pattern appears to be also influenced (shaped) by the geographical distribution of the stock of household education.

The initial disadvantage

The fact that migration has become increasingly less important as an equalizing mechanism for regional disparities (Soto and Torche, 2004) can be explained by the fact that the effect of productivity differentials on the migration decision, which are supposed to guide the migration process, is being annulated by initial disadvantages related to the family background of the potential migrant. The fact that relatively highly educated individuals belonging to poorly educated households observe attractive potential wage gaps means that rural-urban migration has the potential to benefit rural households and movers by allowing to increase their expected wages and, in this way, to reduce regional disparities. However, the structural impact of the household education on the migration probability predicts that those individuals, even when facing attractive potential wage differentials, will have extremely reduced migration probabilities in case of having the initial disadvantage of belonging to a poorly educated household. Unfortunately, the initial disadvantages related to the household background determines that the one who is migrating is not always the one who could profit most from labour market differentials, but the one who is not constrained by its household. The big issue is that both circumstances, on the one hand, to observe high-potential wage differentials and on the other, to be constrained by the low level of education of its households, come together. Thus, the only way to promote an equalizing rural-urban flow is by reducing the household dependence of the potential migrant.

Unemployment and probability models

Ignoring unemployment in the analysis may bias the estimates if unemployment affects movers and stayers unequally after controlling for observed and unobserved characteristics. The inclusion of unemployment would additionally introduce a second selectivity process. However, given the overall low rates of unemployment for the underlying population in 2006 (ranging from 3.5% to 7.7%) it is safe to conclude that unemployment does not affect the fundamental findings of this study. In order to prove the validity of this assumption, Table C.4 in the Appendix shows results of the structural models, including and excluding unemployed potential migrants. The evidence shows that ignoring unemployment is not a big issue, and it is therefore possible to extend with some precaution the main findings of this study to the labour-market participants at origin.

3.6 Conclusions

Based on the idea that migration is an investment decision (Becker, 1962 and Sjaastad, 1962), this paper uses an endogenous switching regression model to determine whether migrant workers are somehow selected according to their observed and unobserved characteristics. The estimation procedure allows to obtain a non-endogenous potential wage differential between origin and destination for each worker with control for the selectivity process involved in the migration decision (to stay or to move). On average, the effect of self-selection on expected incomes is about 36% and 4% for workers originating from rural and urban communes respectively. Thus, ignoring the selection process involved in the migration decision would strongly underestimate the potential wage differential for those originating from rural communes. As a consequence, the effect of productivity differentials on migration would be miscalculated. Moreover, the results are robust across thresholds and model specifications.

Evidence has been found that the potential wage differential strongly determines the probability to move, but only when the differential reaches some determined threshold for individuals with mean characteristics (about 0.5 and 0.3 log-points for workers originating from rural and urban communes respectively). This evidence supports the Neoclassical Economic Theory approach in the sense that potential wage differentials determine migration and can be seen as an investment decision. However, the potential wage differential for most individuals is relatively small compared to the migration costs. This explains why migration is a rare phenomenon being unable to reduce regional disparities.

This paper simultaneously uses the main idea of the New Economics of Labour Migration Theory, considering migration as a household decision (Stark and Bloom, 1985 and Stark 1993). Furthermore, it shows that migration not only depends on individual characteristics, but strongly relies on the household education. In this sense, households matter not only for their composition itself, but also for their intrinsic capacity to generate welfare.

The fact that migration has become increasingly less important as an equalizing mechanism for regional disparities (Soto and Torche, 2004) can be explained by the fact that the effect of productivity differentials on the migration decision, which are supposed to guide the migration process, is being annulled by initial disadvantages related to the family background of the potential migrant. The fact that relatively highly educated individuals belonging to poorly educated households observe attractive potential wage gaps means that rural-urban migration has the potential to benefit rural households and movers by allowing an increase in their expected wages and, in this way, to reduce vulnerability. However, the structural impact of the household education on the migration probability predicts that those individuals, even when facing attractive potential wage differentials, will have extremely reduced migration probabilities in the case of having the initial disadvantage of belonging to a poorly educated household. Unfortunately, the initial disadvantages related to the household background determines that the migrant is not always the one who could profit most from labour market differentials, but rather the one who is not constrained by its household. The big issue is that both circumstances, on the one hand, observe high-potential wage differentials and on the other, to be constrained by the low level of education of its households, come together. Thus, the only way to promote an equalizing rural-urban flow is by reducing the household dependence of the potential migrant.

This study also reveals an interesting conclusion regarding how women (relative to men) are intrinsically motivated to move towards rural communes or stay there. At the same time, due to labour market differentials, women are more likely to move into urban areas or remain there. Such decomposition of the gender-related effects shows the advantages of using a structural model approach.

Finally, this study suggests that supporting the supply side in the rural economy is not the only way to achieve convergence across the territory. Subsidies aimed at reducing migration costs can be also considered under a framework oriented to encourage migration as an effective mechanism to reallocate labour between communes.

Essay 4 - Determinants of student achievements in the primary education in Paraguay[iv]

Abstract

The idea that schooling scores depend on a combination of family background characteristics, ability and school-institutional related variables is quite clear. Regarding the issue of intergenerational transmission of inequality in the educational system, the degree in which a better institutional performance of the school service can compensate problems originated in the family background is crucial. Through the estimation of a reduced form equation for selected scores, we investigate the impact of institutional performance on scores after controlling for family background and individual characteristics. We do this by using a novel data set and an OLS and quantile regression approach to analyze how heterogeneous the process of score generation can be. By providing integral health solutions, minimizing malnutrition and providing ideal conditions in the classroom, training teachers can impact positively on low and mean learning outcomes, thus contributing to an improved educational quality and breaking cycles of intergenerational transmission of inequality. Increasing learning above-median outcomes only strengthens the transmission of inequality. Consequently, the equality approach should focus on trying to improve the bottom tail of the score distributions. Our results show that this can be significantly reached by closing gaps in the training of teachers, improving classroom conditions, health and nutrition.

iv Based on a joint work with Thomas Otter,. This study was published as background paper for the Regional Human Development Report for Latin America and the Caribbean 2010: "Acting on the future: Breaking the intergenerational transmission of inequality."

4.1 Introduction

This paper addresses the question: why and how does an education system fail to provide its students with quality education? To find the answers, schools are one of the first places to search. In Paraguay, education quality is not constrained by the amount of expenditure because the country is spending a larger share of GDP than other Latin American countries and teacher salary levels or expenditure per student are also above the Latin American average. However, the qualifications of teachers, their performance within the classroom, the quality of textbooks and materials and the motivational aspects of pupils seem to make up a recipe which leads to poor educational quality.

We propose to estimate the impact of the different vectors on schooling achievements (Glewwe and Kremer, 2006) as a whole and in a second approach using quantile regressions (quantiles of levels of achievements). Quantile regressions will indicate whether the impact of each explanatory variable changes along the score's distribution or not. Learning achievement indices can be ranked by school stratification. By doing so, we are able to analyze to what extent the differentiation by schools and by socio-economic sectors contribute to score's inequality. To achieve this, we use an inequality measure, traditionally used to measure income inequality.

4.2 Education in Paraguay – an overview

Primary education lays the foundations for a wide range of competencies, mainly comprehensive reading, basic mathematical reasoning, the ability to do homework, or to work as part of a group. Students who do not master these abilities get stuck at a primary level, or if even enrolled at a secondary level, cannot move forward and eventually drop out of high school. Students from poor family backgrounds are especially affected by these limitations. For example, average national rates of repetition are estimated between 17 and 27% for first grade, but are practically double (30 to 50%) for the poorer half of the students' population (Schiefelbein and Brunstein, 2003). Furthermore, these high repetition levels (and their associated low achievement) have been almost constant since at least the 1980s (Zea-Barriga et al., 1981, 37; Schiefelbein and McGinn, 1980).

Results both from the SNEPE testing system and the UNESCO Adult literacy survey confirm low achievement levels in primary education (which generates high repetition rates). SNEPE scores show that less than half of Grade 3 students can understand a brief text (less than 50 words) and that, eventually, only a third of the Grade 6 students will understand a 100-word paragraph in a front-page article of a national newspaper (Schiefelbein and Brunstein, 2003). In each case rural children (from families who are in the lower half of the income distribution) are achieving below the national average. Besides, the UNESCO Adult literacy survey found that only two thirds of the Paraguayan urban population sampled between 15-34 years old selected five or more right answers in a 7-item test rated as easy to answer ("literal" identifications). This score suggests that only half of the sample knew the correct answer for at least 5 of the 7 items (net score near 50%), the balance is close to the result of random success (Schiefelbein and Brunstein, 2003).

Low achievement levels in primary education in Paraguay may be linked to a lack of access to pre-school for children from poor family backgrounds. "Investment in early childhood education is of key importance for building a strong foundation for lifelong learning and to ensure equitable access to learning opportunities later in school" (OECD, 2002: p.182). Paraguay has a high "net pre-school enrolment rate", but there may be few opportunities for children from low income families to attend pre-school (Table 4.1). Lack of resources is another possible cause; therefore, data on expenditure is analyzed in the next section to verify whether resources are an effective constraint to delivering education of the required quality.

Paraguay provides universal access to the first grade of primary school[104] and keeps the newcomers enrolled for six or more years, but only 64% of each cohort finish primary education because teaching low-income students is ineffective and many students repeat grades.[105]

---

104 This figure is sometimes questioned, but Household Survey information on access is 98.3% while the Ministry of Education reports 99.4%.

105 The analysis is focused on the "access to first grade of primary school" because the high coverage now offered in Paraguay reduces the reliability of usual indicators. For example, the "literacy rate" (self-assessment reported to the Census interviewer) is near 100% and the "Net Enrolment Rate" (for the 7-12 age group) is an ambiguous average of a distribution of single age rates (the range limits for "Enrolment Rates by single ages" in ages 7 to 12 are 89.3 to 99.4%). The graduation rate from sixth grade has an upper limit near 64% (some 60% enter secondary education according to the Household Survey data).

Table 4.1: Enrolment rates and school expectancy in 2000

Country	Years and range of high enrolment[1]		Net enrolment rates by age			School expectancy		
			<4	<5<14	<15<19	Less than upper sec.	Upper sec.	Tertiary
Paraguay	5 years	G. 7-11	48.4	98.3	57.3	9.2	1.4	0.6
Brazil	8 years	G. 7-14	24.6	90.1	78	10.9	2.6	0.9
Chile	9 years	G. 6-14	23.6	92.7	66.7	8.4	3.5	1.7
Mexico	7 years	G. 6-12	35.5	94.8	41	9.4	1.4	1
Uruguay*	9 years	G. 6-14	23.5	97.8	60.7	9.9	2.4	1.8
Avg. OECD	12 years	G. 4-15	63.8	97.9	77.3	9.4	3.6	2.5

Notes: [1]At which over 90 % of the population are enrolled. Lower secondary usually consists of three to six years of schooling. Upper secondary could be terminal (preparing for a direct entry into working life) or preparatory. School expectancy must be compared with the length of "primary and lower secondary education" in each country.

Sources: OECD, Education at a Glance, 2002. OECD Indicators 2002: pp. 220-1.

Almost 97% of children aged seven are "timely" enrolled. Dropping out begins between the ages of 9 and 11 when 10% of the cohort leaves school. Dropping out at the age of 11 or younger corresponds mainly to students that need personalized attention to learn.[106] The impact of economic pressures begins at the age of 13 when 12% of the age group drops out. Dropping out accounts for 9% of the group aged 14 and similar rates are observed for the subsequent age groups. About 90% of the students remained enrolled in primary school for at least six years. However, only 60% of each population cohort enrols in first year of secondary education. This attrition is linked to family income and education levels and poor reading comprehension that is associated with repetition. Both causes may also be linked to not attending pre-school education.

Enrolment data show that primary education coverage increased by about five percentage points relative to the previous decade (UNESCO-OREALC, 2001: p.316) even though enrolment data could have an error of up to 3% (be-

106 About 10% of the population needs personalized attention (and facilities) for learning. Most Paraguayan schools cannot offer such special care. Therefore, students that need special attention either do not enrol or drop out early. There are economic variables linked to those earlier drop-outs involving special needs. In a richer country an equivalent student would not end up dropping out partly because in some cases parents would pay for special attention, in other cases the schools would have the economic and human resources needed to deal with such cases, and in part because both parents and teachers would identify the problem better and earlier (in those cases where what is needed is not so much additional special resources as simply a proper diagnosis). Depending on the magnitude of the problem, the unit cost per student (to provide them a fair instruction) may be three to ten times higher than the current average unit costs.

cause enrolments may be over-reported or age dispersal may be underestimated). However, figures from different sources are consistent enough. The 2001 Household Survey shows that only 1.7% of the group aged between 10-15 years did not enrol in school (DGEEC, 2000) and therefore at least 98.3% had access to grade one in primary education. Hence, the probable level of error in enrolment data does not significantly affect the analysis of students' flows (carried out by comparing the net enrolment rates for each single age) presented below.

Teachers make a student repeat Grade 1 when the student cannot decode simple words. Most Grade 1 students who are aged eight or older are repeating Grade 1 because there was timely enrolment of 96.5% of the group aged seven years. At most 5070 newcomers who enrolled in 1999 in Grade 1 at the age of 8 ([100.0-96.5%] multiplied by 143,843) and 869 who enrolled in 1999 in Grade 1 at the age of 9 (0.6% multiplied by 141,694) should not be counted as repeaters.[107] However, some 10% of the students aged 6 that enrolled in 1998 (some 98,000, because the figure was 99,237 in 1999) may be repeaters in 1999. For the sake of simplicity both "corrections" have not been included in the "low estimate" of first grade repetition presented in the next paragraph.[108]

A "low estimate" of repetition in Grade 1 (data from 1999) corresponds to students of 8 years and older (given than 96.5% of the seven year olds enrolled on time). The 34,578 repeaters represent 17% of repeaters in Grade 1, but some have repeated several times. In fact, the total first grade repetition is 57,615 student-years (the number of "over-aged students" multiplied by the number of "extra years") and represents a high cost in resources (because most of those students should have learned to "decode a short written text" in one year, and be promoted to second grade). The "low estimate" of the repetition rate (Table D.3 in the Appendix) slightly exceeds the repetition rates reported by the school principals (UNESCO-OREALC, 2001: p.318), but is below the 20.2% failure in first grade reported in 1999 (PNUD, 2003: p.172).

A "high estimate" of repetition in Grade 1 assumes that the share of newcomers aged between 5 and 8 years is near constant over time (according to dis-

107 This assumes that 100% of the cohort was enrolled and that (100-99.4%) dropped out after one or two years of schooling.

108 There is a difference between the "number of repeaters in grade 1 of primary as of 1999" and the "total number of years repeated by students that are in grade 1 of primary in 1999". Most children with normal talent and behaviour would not repeat grade 1 more than three or four years. However, parents with children with learning difficulties or requiring special assistance may keep them more years in first grade (because there may be no work opportunities for them or consider the school as a low-cost caring alternative).

tance to school, sex, talent distribution, or traditions) and that the percentages– for each of these four ages (regarding each population)– should add up close to 100% (newcomers should be in a range of 97.7 to 99.4 or 100% of the population of the normal entrance age according to the Household Survey and institutional data). Given that over 90% of newcomers are aged 6 or 7 years and the small difference in both populations (the difference between 145,878 and 143,843 being less than 2%) the 7 year old group is used as the basis.

The repetition figures for Paraguay are well above the levels in OECD countries, but they are similar to the averages in other Latin American countries (UNESCO, 2008: p.4 and p.44; Wolff et al., 2002). The rate of repetition is usually low (about 4 or 5%) in schools for students in urban non-marginal areas, and rather high (between 30 and 50%) in urban-marginal and rural areas. If Paraguayan schools were split into two halves (according to family income), the national average would correspond to half of the sum of the repetition rates of the wealthier and poorer halves. For example, repetition would approach 30% in poorer areas if the rate were 4% in the wealthier areas according to the "low estimate" for Paraguayan schools in 1999 – and the corresponding figures would be 50 and 4 for the "high estimate". These assumptions (for wealthier and deprived areas) – and the implication on the impact of teaching methods – suggest the need for estimating repetition by family income levels.

If most of the average students enrolled in Grade 1 are students from the lower half of the income distribution, their teachers will have a tough task teaching such heterogeneous classes. High repetition constrains the education levels of children from low-income families (few of them reach secondary education) and increases the age-heterogeneity in classrooms reducing the effectiveness of frontal teaching. Furthermore, repetition is also linked to dropping out (and to family income levels) as discussed in the rest of this section.

In general, dropping out is generated by several causes. It is probable that children with physical or mental limitations are forced to drop out first because the regular system does not deliver the special attention that they need. Most of these early dropouts (aged 11 and 12) would correspond to students with special attention needs that are not available in the regular schools where they are enrolled, although only one out of ten (1% of the population) needs to be in special institutions outside the regular system of education. Dropping out generated by other reasons –mainly pressure to contribute to the family income– really begins around the ages of 13 and 14 years when some 10% of that age group drops out. This group of dropouts was enrolled for some eight years, although some dropped out temporarily during harvest periods. Paraguayan data suggest that these students did not complete primary education because they repeated several times due to poor achievement.

In summary, the school system has built enough space to take care of each new population cohort reaching school age, but substantial repetition linked to poor achievement and eventual dropping out distorts the enrolment pyramid reducing the access to higher grades. Repetition and dropping out (more recurrent in students from low-income families) generate a large gap between newcomer students to grade 1 in primary education and the subset starting secondary education. Grade repetition and early dropouts eventually reduce the number of children from low-income families enrolled in secondary or higher education. Repeaters and dropouts tend to be members of low-income families.

Despite the significant progress Paraguay has achieved in recent years regarding access to education and school permanence, the country still faces great challenges. These include the problems of internal efficiency, quality in learning and equity. For instance, retention rates indicate that half of school children finish their 6th grade without having to repeat any grade (44% in rural areas and 62% in urban areas). Regarding children's learning, the low scores achieved in the SNEPE's tests of 2004 (3rd grade: 54% for language and literature and 58% for math; 6th grade: 60% for language and literature and 63% for math) show that the quantitative growth of the system is not ensuring an adequate level of learning.

In Paraguay, education quality is not severely constrained by the amount of expenditure because the country spends a larger share of GDP than other Latin American countries and teachers' salary levels or expenditure per student are also above the Latin American average. However, the qualifications of teachers, their classroom performance, the quality of textbooks and materials and the motivational aspects of pupils seem to form a recipe which results in poor educational quality.

Total expenditures on education as a percentage of GDP in Paraguay are higher compared with other countries of the Southern Cone, Mexico and even the average (Table 4.2). The percentages for upper secondary are over twice as high than all other countries, and only expenditures in tertiary education are below the figures for Chile and for the average OECD country. However, given that GDP figures may be underestimated, this conclusion should be eventually revised. Furthermore, there is a balanced contribution of both public and private sources (Table 4.2). Funding for education is provided both by direct public expenditure (4.8% of GDP) and through private spending in educational institutions (3.7%). Paraguay spends on public education the same as the median spending of "countries with high human development" and above the 4.2% in "medium human development countries" where Paraguay is included (UNDP, 2003: p.93).

Table 4.2: Total expenditure on education as percentage of GDP in 1999

Percentage of GDP spent by educational levels and sector

Country	Pre-Upper Secondary	Upper secondary	Tertiary	Total[1]	Public	Private	Estimated total[2]
Paraguay	4.0	2.8	1.5	8.5	4.8	3.7	8.5
Argentina	3.2	0.8	1.1	5.8	4.5	1.3	5.8
Brazil[3]	3.4	0.6	1.1	5.1	5.1	n.a.	6.2
Chile	3.6	1.4	2.2	7.2	4.1	3.1	7.2
Mexico	3.3	0.8	1.1	5.2	4.4	0.8	5.2
Uruguay[3]	1.9	0.5	0.6	3.0	2.9	n.a.	4.0
Avg. OECD	2.3	1.3	1.6	5.8	4.6	1.1	5.8

Notes: [1]This includes undistributed expenditure and advanced research programs. [2]This includes estimated private expenditure similar to the average OECD. [3]This includes only direct public expenditure by educational levels.

Sources: OECD, Education at a Glance, 2002; OECD, Indicators, 2002: pp. 170-72.

These figures show a comparatively high level of resources being allocated to education. However, it is necessary to confirm whether funds are used to pay teachers suitable salary levels and to assess the level of expenditure per student comparing it with the expenditure per student in other Latin American countries.

Mid-career salaries for Paraguayan teachers relative to GDP per-capita are high compared with the countries of the Southern Cone and Mexico (Table 4.3). Teacher salaries is a key variable for attracting good candidates for initial teacher training, keeping trained teachers in the profession, and reducing the real school calendar for time spent on strike. A high salary should have a positive impact on these three aspects and should also improve students' achievement, reduce repetition and raise the quality of Human Capital in Paraguay. On the other hand, teacher salaries make up near 90% of the cost of providing education in Paraguay, making this variable a crucial element in decision making in education. There is a trade-off between better-paid teachers and a balanced education budget.

"Salaries and working conditions of teachers, including starting salaries and pay scales, and the costs incurred by individuals in becoming teachers, compared to salaries and costs in other high skill occupations are key factors in determining the supply of qualified teachers" (OECD, 2002: p.332). The comparison of teachers' salaries to GDP per-capita provides an indicator of the relative value of teachers' salaries and also of the affordability for countries (Table 4.3). Paraguayan teachers obtain salaries that are equivalent from 2.0 to 3.1 times the GDP per-capita in the country. These ratios are better than Brazil (1.5 and 2.4), Chile (1.4), Mexico (1.6 and 2.1) or even Uruguay (1.6 assuming full-time workload). The Paraguayan ratio is also higher than the average OECD country (1.3). In fact, "the ratio of the average upper secondary teacher's salary to GDP per-capita is the second of all WEI [World Education Indicators] countries at 3.13 and above all OECD countries" (OECD-WEI, 2003, 137).

In Paraguay, teachers' salaries increase with the level of education (Table 4.3). There is no increment linked with years of experience, while such an increment is near 40% in Brazil, 10% in Chile, 30% in Mexico, 20% in Uruguay, 90% in New Zealand and 40% in the average OECD country. The salary in Secondary Education (with training) is 60% higher than the salary in Primary Education.

Table 4.3: Ratio of teacher salaries after 15 years of experience to GDP per-capita in 2000[1]

Country	Wages in primary education (with training)			Wages in secondary education (with training)		
	Starting	15 Years	Ratio to GDP/P	Starting	15 Years	Ratio to GDP/P
Paraguay	8,874	8,874	2.0	13,911	13,911	3.1
Brazil	7,420	10,176	1.5	14,820	16,240	2.4
Chile	10,716	12,038	1.4	10,716	12,038	1.4
Mexico	11,235	14,824	1.6	14,383	18,760	2.1
Uruguay	5,749	6,891	0.8	5,749	6,891	0.8
New Zealand	17,354	33,653	1.7	17,354	33,653	1.7
Avg. OECD	21,469	29,407	1.3	22,727	31,221	1.4

Note: [1]Equivalent US dollars converted using purchasing power parities PPP. Salaries based on a 20 hour per week workload. Most teachers hold two positions. Figures in the last column should be further revised given that the GDP estimations are distorted for certain years. This includes estimated private expenditure similar to the average OECD.

Sources: OECD, Education at a Glance, 2002; OECD, Indicators, 2002: p.339.

This percentage is similar to the situation in Brazil (also 60%), and higher than in Mexico (30%) or the other countries presented in Table 4.3. In the average OECD country the salary in Secondary Education (with training) is only 10% higher than the salary in Primary Education. Of course, salaries per teaching hour in Paraguay are also higher in secondary education, since secondary teachers (as in most countries) are required to teach fewer hours than primary teachers. Even though the Paraguayan expenditure per primary student is the lowest, the country invests in each student a higher percentage of its GDP per-capita than the rest of the countries of the Southern Cone and Mexico (Table 4.4).

The analysis of the "expenditure per primary student" indicator is tricky because the short-term and long-term effects must be taken into account. For example, the expenditure per primary student depends on the salary paid to the teacher, but a sudden salary increment cannot change the training of the teacher. The same teacher will still be teaching tomorrow, in spite of receiving more money than today.

> "The expenditure per student indicator shows direct public and private expenditure on educational institutions in relation to the number of full-time equivalent students enrolled in each level. . . . The variation in expenditure on education per student may reflect not only variation in the material resources provided to students (e.g., variations in the ratio of students to teaching staff) but also variation in relative salary levels" (OECD, 2002: p.147).

Teachers' salaries have a major impact in overall unit costs given the traditionally labour-intensive teaching processes. Increments in salaries have a proportional increment in the expenditure per student. Student-teacher ratios also have an important effect; Paraguay had 21 students per primary teacher in 1996, therefore an increment up to a 30 student teacher ratio would reduce the "annual expenditure per student" (a proxy of the unit cost) by 30%. On the other hand, a drop in enrolments may lead to a significant increase in spending on education per student (OECD, 2002: p.150).

The annual expenditure per student in Paraguay increases significantly with the level of education as it happens throughout the OECD countries (see the OECD averages in the last row in Table 4.4). At the secondary education level, the annual expenditure per student is 1.8 times the expenditure per student at the primary education level (80% higher). This increment is higher than in other countries of the Southern Cone (1.1 to 1.4), Mexico (1.4) and the OECD average (1.3). At the tertiary level, the annual expenditure per student is 6.2 times the expenditure per student at the primary education level. This increment is lower than the increment in Brazil (14.2), but higher than the rest of the countries of the Southern Cone (ranging from 2.2 to 4.1), Mexico (4.4) and the OECD average (2.2).

Table D.3 in the Appendix shows a summary of descriptive schooling statistics in Paraguay.

Table: 4.4: Annual expenditure per student by level of education and as a percentage of GDP per-capita in 1999[1]

Country	Expenditure per student by level of education			Expenditure as a percentage of GDP per-capita		
	Primary	Secondary	Tertiary	Primary	Secondary	Tertiary
Paraguay	877	1,545	5,465	20	35	125
Argentina	1,629	2,327	5,606	13	19	46
Brazil	956	1,100	13,567	14	16	195
Chile	1,701	1,941	6,911	20	22	80
Mexico	1,096	1,480	4,789	13	18	57
Uruguay	1,000	1,275	2,239	11	14	25
Avg. OECD	4,148	5,465	9,210	19	25	44

Note [1]Equivalent US dollars converted using purchasing power parities PPP.

Sources: OECD, Education at a Glance, 2002; OECD, Indicators, 2002: pp.158-59.

4.3 The data

We use three different data sets, namely the Paraguayan household survey (*Encuesta Permanente de Hogares* – EPH 2005), the World Education Indicators' Survey of Primary Schools (WEI-SPS) prepared by UNCESO (data from 2006), and data from the SNEPE (Sistema Nacional de Evaluación del Proceso Educativo) survey in Paraguay in 2003. The WEI-SPS survey was applied to students in grade 4 and SNEPE exams were applied to students in grade 3 as well as to teachers in training (future teachers). The idea of this research was to use the learning outcomes score variable provided by the SNEPE data base as the dependent variable and build up a combined data set with information from SNEPE, EPH and WEI-SPS for the explanatory variables.

The SNEPE data base provides information on the results of mathematics and reading / writing tests as a percentage of correct answers and as the associated qualification in school grades. We used the mathematics and communication scores in its pure form (non-logarithmic) as dependent variables. In general, the way our model is specified, it can be understood as a reduced form specification where the coefficients change in their scope according to the specification of the production function.

4.4 Previous research

Since the mid-1960s, a vast amount of literature has unfolded in the United States and Europe in an attempt to estimate some production function of learning. Hanushek (1997) accounts for 376 published estimates of US education production functions from 89 separate articles published in peer reviewed journals or books until 1994.

Apart from the US and European evidence, there are also several studies on education production functions in developing countries, summarized e.g. in Hanushek (1997) and Glewwe (2002). While many of the older studies for developing countries have been criticized for their lack of methodological and data quality, several more recent studies have presented convincing evidence on education production functions for countries in Latin America, Africa, and Asia (see the references in Glewwe 2002). In particular, several studies use data from randomized trials to estimate the impact of distinct educational policies on student performance, most recently in Kenya (see the overview by Kremer 2003), and quasi-experimental evidence on class-size effects exists for South Africa (Case and Deaton 1999), as well as Israel (Angrist and Lavy 1999). While nearly all of these studies are confined to individual countries, recent internationally comparable evidence exists for several countries in francophone sub-Saharan Africa (Michaelowa 2001) and for several newly industrializing countries in East Asia (Wößmann 2003).

4.5 Approach and methodology

Glewwe and Kremer (2006), propose to estimate the production function for learning that may lead to future earnings according to a structural relationship that can be depicted as:

$$A = a(S, Q, C, H, I) \qquad (1)$$

where A represents the skills learned (achievement), S represents the years of schooling, Q represents a vector of school and teacher characteristics (quality), C represents a vector of child characteristics (including "innate ability"), H represents a vector of household characteristics, and I represents a vector of school inputs under the control of parents, such as children's daily attendance and purchase of textbooks and other school supplies (endogenous vector). Based on the data available in Paraguay, primarily a national survey on educational achievements for grade 4 (see below), we propose to estimate the reduced form relationship.

$$A = k(C, H, L, EP) \quad (2)$$

Where all vectors are exogenous, L represents the local community characteristics and EP the education policies. L and EP may interact to determine the quality (Q) of a school and even the prices (P) of educational inputs such as fees.

$$Q = q(L, EP) \quad (3)$$

$$P = p(L, P) \quad (4)$$

In principle, a reduced form equation can be estimated as A=h(Q,C,H,P), but because of the impossibility of getting all prices (P) and schools characteristic which determine quality (Q) and given our available data, we abandoned attempts to estimate the reduced form and we estimate the above reduced form relationship which directly links education policies and local characteristics to our available educational outputs.

In our case, achievements and skills can be operationalized throughout scores of standardized tests for the areas of reading / writing and mathematics. We propose to estimate the impact of the different vectors on schooling achievements as a whole and in a second approach via quantile estimations (quantiles of levels of achievements). Quantile regressions will indicate whether each explanatory variable's effect changes along the score's distribution or not. Additionally, we are able to analyze to what extent differentiation by schools and by socio-economic sectors contribute to score's inequality.

To achieve this, we use an inequality measure, traditionally used to measure income inequality: the Theil 2 Index. The Theil 2 measure -the mean logarithmic deviation measure- is defined as:

$$T_2 = \frac{1}{N}\sum_{i=1}^{N} \ln\left(\frac{u}{A_i}\right)$$

Where A_i represents the student i test score, N represents the total number of students and u represents the mean test score of the distribution. This index is zero for the case of perfect equality, approaches infinity in the case of perfect inequality, and can take intermediate values between the two.

We choose this inequality index because it satisfies a set of axioms and properties that are convenient when measuring inequality: *symmetry* (the measure is unchanged if there is a permutation of test scores between two persons; this principle is also called the *anonymity* principle); *replication invariance* (the measure is unchanged if the population is doubled, tripled, and so forth), *mean independence* (the measure is unchanged if all scores in the distribution are multiplied by a scalar); and the *Pigou-Dalton Principle* (the inequality measure increases with any regressive shift in the (same total) scores from low to high performers. The Gini Index also satisfies these properties so we will report results of both indices further ahead.

4.5.1 Quantile approach – Median regression

Consider the following distribution function from a random variable Y

$$F(y) = \Pr(Y \leq y) \tag{5}$$

For any $\tau \epsilon (0,1)$ the quantile of Y is defined as:

$$Q(\tau) = inf\ \{y: F(y) \geq \tau\} \tag{6}$$

The quantile function gives a complete characterization of Y. $Q(0.5)$ is the median, the first quartile is $Q(0.25)$, the first decile is $Q(0.1)$ and so on. We can now write (3) in a different way. Let $x_i, i = 1, \ldots, n$ a $(K \times 1)$ vector of explanatory variables, then:

$$F_{u\tau}(\tau - x_i'\beta_\tau | x_i) = Pr\ (y_i \leq \tau | x_i) \tag{7}$$

This equation is equivalent to:

$$Y_i = x_i'\beta_\tau + u_{\tau i} \tag{8}$$

Where the only constraint is that $Q_\tau(u_{\tau i}|x_i) = 0$ and the distribution of this error term left unspecified. From this we now write the linear conditional quantile function as:

$$Q_\tau(\tau|X = x) = x_i'\beta_\tau \quad (9)$$

Where β_τ can be estimated solving:

$$\beta_\tau = arg \min_{\beta \epsilon R^k} \sum_{i=1}^{n} \rho_\tau(y_{i-} x_i'\beta_\tau)$$

Where $\rho_\tau(u) = u(\rho_\tau - I(u < 0))$ is the piecewise linear "check function" and $I()$ is the indicator function. The quantile regression estimator achieves a more complete description of the conditional distribution of Ygiven $X = x$. The partial derivate of the conditional quantile of y (see(7)) with respect to one of the regressors, *j-th*, could be interpreted as the marginal change in the $\tau - th$ quantile due to a marginal change in the *j-th* regressor. Note that this marginal effect is related with τ and not with some particular individual, which changes their $\tau - th$ quantile simultaneously when some value of their explanatory variable changes.

There is a major advantage using Quantile regression. We can detect and deal with the plausible heteroskedasticity in the data allowing different slopes for each conditional quantile in the wage distribution. Using the method suggested by Koenker and Bassett (1978, 1982) to obtain the standard errors, Rogers (1992) reports that these standard errors are suitable in the homoskedastic case but that they look to be understated in the presence of heteroskedastic errors. Accepting the heteroskedastic nature of our data, we proceed to bootstrap the estimated coefficients in order to obtain the standard errors relaxing the homoskedastic assumption and improving our inference power.[109]

The median regression is also more robust than an OLS regression in presence of outliers and a difference of Heckman ML estimators, it does not relay on the normality of the residuals because the estimation is only influenced by the local behaviour of the conditional distribution near the specified quantile.

---

[109] The bootstrap is a computational intensive procedure for assessing uncertainty in estimation, in which through resampling data replaces mathematical analysis. We use the bootstrap to attach a standard error of the estimated parameter.

4.5.2 Some comments on applied econometrics

The first estimation method applied in this paper is a linear OLS regression for survey data. This estimation technique relies on the normal distribution of residuals with zero mean. The fact that unobserved characteristics could be correlated with some explanatory variable potentially introduces a bias in our estimates. In order to avoid this source of bias, we exploit our data base in order to minimize the possibility of observed characteristics remaining in our residual, and in this way reducing the probability of an error of specification (omitted variable problem).

Although extensive reviews of related literature exist,[110] much controversy remains over what conventional estimates of education production functions can and do tell about the causal relation of student performance, for example with respect to the effectiveness of class-size (Krueger, 2003).

The main data base used in our work is SNEPE, which identifies cluster (school id) and strata (public-urban, private-urban, public-rural and private-rural), and therefore we adopt the sample design in order to optimize the precision of our estimators. In order to incorporate other indicators, we merge our main data base with the mean values for each variable of interest at the district level, provided by the WEI-SPS and EPH data bases.

This methodology is more powerful than the usual (frequently cited in literature) weighted OLS regression approach, given that it controls for cluster correlations. Control for cluster correlations in our case basically means that we take into account the fact that in certain sectors we might have several schools that are quite homogeneous. In this case, variation will not be a pure (100%) random effect. Ignoring these cluster effects would imply considering each observation as independent, which would create artificially higher variation coefficients, an underestimation of standard errors and possibly accepting statistically significant results when in reality they do not exist. Standard errors in our estimation are robust because they are clustered at the school level.

For quantile regressions we used the bootstrapping procedure considering the clustered structure of our data and ran these with R software.[111] This way we basically get almost the same statistical rigor in quantile regressions as in OLS, via bootstrapping with 500 replications.[112]

---

110 About the specification and interpretation of education production functions, Hanushek (1986; 2002) offers an excellent discussion.

111 We use the *quantreg* package developed by Roger Koenker.

112 Efron and Tibshirani (1993) demonstrates that 200 replication provides enough information to properly compute the standard deviations of our estimates.

The bootstrapping procedure which takes into account the clustered design of our database, additionally allows to avoid any assumption about the underlying score distributions. Thus, it is a proper way to relax those exigent distributional assumptions concerning the nature of the residual structure in the regression models given the fact that our data set contains variables at different aggregation levels.

4.6 Results

Tables D.1 and D.2 in Appendix show descriptive statistics of our joint data base of EPH, WEI and SNEPE data, expressed as quintile means. Note that since we have no income data in our data base, quintiles refer to test scores (T); this is true for the descriptive statistics below as well as for the quantile regressions further below in the text.

We have divided our results into four different groups: students' personal characteristics (C) such as age, gender, perspectives indicator; family background (F) such as parental education, language, coeducational vocation of parents; Local Characteristics (L) such as district average child sickness rate, district average health insurance rate, district undernourishment rate and urban/rural public/private status; and Educational Policies Variables (EP) such as school language, optimal classroom conditions and school size, which are treated as exogenous. Since there is no self-selection into the sample as 3rd grade schooling is compulsory,[113] least-squares estimates should represent causal family-background effects. It helps to clarify in advance what the estimates of the coefficients on the family-background variables stand for. Given the technical constraints on the pedagogical process, the size of the effect of any family-background characteristic on students' educational performance should be the same everywhere. If this is not the case, this implies that there must be differences in how the school system works.

According to Wößmann (2003), as to the main family-background effects we have the education level attained by the parents, which is strongly related to student performance; the social and economic background of the students in general and families' unobserved aspects of family background, such as parent's motivation or their willingness and capability to help with homework. In general, it seems to be that a larger family-background effect materializes in terms of better educational performance of the children rather than in terms of higher attainment levels.

113 According to data from EPH 2005, the gross enrolment rate for boys and girls aged 8 (official age for 3rd grade) is 97.8% (self-processed data).

Additionally, least-square regression results of student performance on schools' resource endowments and of teacher characteristics, controlling for family-background influences, might suffer from endogeneity bias. The resource endowments that students face may be particularly prone to endogeneity, in that resources and student performance are simultaneously determined by other factors or that the latter is even directly used to determine a reverse causality (Hoxby, 2000). For example, school systems may sort weaker students into smaller classes, giving rise to a negative correlation between performance and the teacher-student ratio in classes (West and Wößmann, 2003). Also, parents of high performing students may choose to move into areas where schools are better resourced, giving rise to a positive performance-resource correlation. None of these correlations say anything about the causal effect of resource endowments on student performance. In short, parents, teachers, schools, and administrators all make choices that may give rise to a non-causal relationship between resources and student performance, so that least-squares estimates of resource effects may be biased.[114] Of course, there are some possibilities to control for this effect. For example, some recent influential studies have tried to avoid endogeneity biases in the class-size estimates by using experimental evidence from the Tennessee Project STAR (Krueger, 1999) and quasi-experimental research design for data from Connecticut (Hoxby, 2000); one of them finding substantial class-size effects while the other finding none at all. Nevertheless, in practice it is almost impossible to control for all possible biases, mainly due to limitations in the data itself.

Tables D.4 and D.5 in the Appendix respectively show results of the OLS baseline and the full specifications, while Tables D.6 and D.7 show results of the same specifications estimated using the quantile regressions technique.

4.6.1 Language (F, EP)

Surprisingly, students from Guaraní speaking families in our data show a higher performance than those from Spanish or other language speaking households. By looking at the tables (ols math, ols com, quant math, quant com), it is clear that the family language effect on communication score concentrates towards the upper tail of the distribution, while for Mathematic scores the effect appears to be more equally distributed and of greater magnitude. This result, contrary to

114 Hoxby (2000) shows that simple least-squares estimates of resource effects are biased upwards in the case of class-size effects in the US state of Connecticut; i.e., the least-squares estimates are biased in the direction of finding positive effects of smaller classes on student performance.

the expected outcomes and inconsistent with other empirical evidence,[115] could be produced by a problem of selective sample design, where schools with a higher native or indigenous background were over-represented, and thus sub-representing at the same time (elite or higher qualified) schools of non-native urban students.[116] Nevertheless, Spanish speaking teachers on average have higher performing students (ceteris paribus) than teachers who speak any other language.

The impact of the language usually spoken in the household is smaller than the impact of the teacher's language. This way we observe that teachers who are teaching in languages other than Guaraní have a negative impact on student performance compared to teachers teaching in Spanish.

The institutional language variable (language spoken by the teacher) is powerful and controls for the language spoken in the household. This way we observe a pure association (correlation and non-causality proved) between the teacher's language and the student's performance. Quantile regressions and OLS show for communication (Spanish) and mathematics a robust impact in all specifications. Our findings could indicate a "low teaching quality" of "native", mostly rural or sub-urban Guaraní speaking teachers. A differentiated teacher's training for non-Spanish speaking teachers might help to improve this situation.

The effect on scores follows an inverted U-shape, where students who are concentrated precisely around the median obtain approximately one score point more than students who are taught in a language other than Spanish. These issues therefore limit the progress of good students, while also precluding the improvement of poorly performing students.

115 For instance, the JICA Report on the Paraguayan education sector (JICA and Instituto Desarrollo, 2004) mentions a double limitation which arises from the dilemma of a population of which at least 75% speak Guaraní as mother tongue but implements (as a teacher) and attends (as a student) a Spanish speaking schooling system. Many pupils do not speak Spanish adequately when entering school and have difficulties keeping pace with the classes; meanwhile teachers whose mother tongue is Guaraní frequently show limited capacities in adequately transmitting curricular contents in Spanish.

116 The number of well-performing urban schools with Spanish speaking teachers is in fact lower than the number of poorly-performing rural, sub-urban and even urban schools. If sub-representation of these generally better performing schools is so low that we get only a very limited number of cases, thus there is space for a random selection of the worst performing Spanish speaking urban schools, which could create this kind of bias.

4.6.2 Under-nutrition (L)

Under-nutrition is defined as the mean district under-nutrition rate and belongs to the local community characteristics (vector L). This variable shows the expected negative outcomes on schooling performance. Given its nature, it can be considered as exogenous from the point of view of households only and only if we suppose that there are local factors that determine the district rates of under-nutrition and the nutrition of each of the children in the district.

Our results clearly show that higher under-nutrition rates impact negatively on schooling performance concerning the median and below. Nevertheless, the impact of nutritional problems is higher in mathematics than in communication. This variable has a U-shaped impact on scores. Since the nutrition variable is a district mean and not individual information, it does not clearly show that nutritional problems might explain poor schooling performance on the average. Nevertheless, it shows that good school performance is immune to nutritional problems basically because we can suppose that good performing students do not suffer problems of under-nutrition. The overall nutritional impact is quite important. School performance of districts with zero under-nutrition is 3 to 6 points higher than the districts with the highest levels of nutritional problems. It is important to keep in mind that the nutritional variable ranks from 0 to 1. We can therefore roughly conclude, for example, that reducing average under-nutrition from 0.5 to 0.4 could improve schooling performance between 0.3 and 0.6 points (according to our data).

Consequently, our data show that poor parents are likely to produce poorly nourished children with low schooling performance, and therefore low human capital accumulation, resulting later on in probable low incomes and ongoing poverty. But given that there also exist spatial patterns of poverty (poorer areas or poverty pockets within better-off areas), under-nutrition can simultaneously have endogenous and exogenous characteristics.

4.6.3 Optimal class room conditions (EP)

This is a constructed variable that includes information provided by the students on the existence of chairs, desks, electricity and the individual feeling of being comfortable in the classroom. Even if this variable seems to have a subjective background, it is objective in the sense that students who do not feel comfortable will not express the opposite feeling. The variable is operationalized as a dummy variable and is robust in OLS and quantiles.[117] Its impact is stronger on mathematics than on communication and homogeneous impacts throughout the distribution, which basically reflects that both good and bad students benefit in a similar way from good classroom conditions. Additionally, if students have varied backgrounds, optimal conditions would be a progressive factor, given that they offer an environment of equality in the classroom for students coming from unequal homes.

4.6.4 Small-scale school (EP)

We have to be quite careful with the interpretation of this variable, given its problems of endogeneity. Small schools are defined following a classification adopted by the Paraguayan educational authority.[118] Small schools can impact the score, but at the same time the score can impact on the school's scale. For example, a small school can in fact benefit the median, but at the same time the scale can be a consequence of better families who select small schools for their children in order to get personalized teaching in small groups; this way a higher score can determine the school's scale. Within our data set, the school size variable is most affected by endogeneity meanwhile the literature cites school scale and class size as the most affected variables.

Thus we discuss their estimates only in terms of correlations. Small schools are associated, on the average, with higher performance. Quantiles show an inverse U shape indicating that students performing at a mean level benefit from attending a small school (according to the official classification from the Ministry of Education). Behind this observation, we might have the fact that small schools offer a less competitive or more familiar environment, which might be a limitation for better performing students or might be the consequence of the existence of small schools for students with whatever kind of inability or small schools as a response to the lack of resources. Whatever the real cause of the inverse U shape may be, small schools seem to be ideal for median performing students. Even if we do not have a strong evidence of causality for this, we can at least state that small schools would do no harm and offer the possibility to create an environment where other variables, positively related to schooling scores, could start to have a positive additional impact.

117 Defined as 1 if the student reports to have adequate chair, desk and ventilation and that he additionally feels comfortable. Only if all four conditions are fulfilled is the dummy 1, otherwise 0 is assigned.

118 For details see http://www.mec.gov.py/cms.

4.6.5 District mean level of health insurance (L)

Our evidence seems to indicate that bad students benefit most from higher district levels of health insurance. We cannot, however, understand our quantile estimate results in a way that once we increase the health insurance level at a given district, students will perform better. We rather should think about it in a way that health insurance rates are part of a more favourable learning environment and contribute to a better performance. So it is not that higher insurance rates make poor performance as bad as it is, but that without the positive impact of higher insurance rates, poor performance rates would be even worse.

4.6.6 Inequality analysis

Estimating inequality of scores and comparing them with the variation of regression coefficients by income quantile allows us to understand to what extent differentiation by schools and by socio-economic sectors contributes to score's inequality.

Table 4.5: Inequality indicators and regression coefficients for mathematic scores

Inequality Index	Q1	Q2	Q3	Q4	Q5
Theil 1	0.04408	0.00659	0.00278	0.00126	0.00125
Theil 2	0.03957	0.00656	0.00277	0.00126	0.00126
Gini	0.15702	0.06499	0.04197	0.0280	0.02811
Spanish speaking teacher	0.80575	0.8656	0.86778	0.88219	0.89165
Classroom conditions	0.84633	0.8825	0.89580	0.90953	0.94688
Small size school	0.17021	0.16318	0.19282	0.26735	0.28568

Source: Own estimates based on joint database EPH 2005 (DGEEC), SNEPE 2003 (MEC) WEI-SPS 2006 (UNESCO).

Tables 4.5 and 4.6 show that, within lower score quintiles, inequality is generally higher for any inequality indicator we use and inequality generally decreases towards higher quintiles. This is entirely true for mathematic scores and is true for quintile 1 to 4 regarding communication scores. Nevertheless, we observe an inequality increase for communication scores in the highest quintile. At the same time, regression coefficients of our three selected institutional (school) variables are higher for higher quintiles, so they have a bigger impact to increase score results.

Table 4.6: Inequality indicators and regression coefficients for communication scores

Inequality Index	Q1	Q2	Q3	Q4	Q5
Theil 1	0.0376	0.0046	0.0026	0.0018	0.0042
Theil 2	0.0337	0.0046	0.0026	0.0018	0.0042
Gini	0.1431	0.0531	0.0400	0.0331	0.0513
Spanish speaking teacher	0.7958	0.8594	0.8703	0.8813	0.9038
Classroom conditions	0.8429	0.8860	0.8981	0.9164	0.9376
Small size school	0.2034	0.2046	0.2012	0.2533	0.2702

Source: Own estimates based on joint database EPH 2005 (DGEEC), SNEPE 2003 (MEC) WEI-SPS 2006 (UNESCO).

If score inequality is to be reduced most efficiently, considering the complete distribution, increasing scores in lower quintiles, we clearly find the opposite situation here. In a way, learning outcomes even seem to be "regressive". So even if it's true that improving the impact of our selected variables would have a positive effect on scores, we would only reduce inequality if this happens for low income quantiles, but not for the higher ones. If we improve the impact of our institutional variables throughout the complete distribution, inequality might even increase or at least remain the same.

4.6.7 Test of robustness

Our reduced form assumes exogeneity of our explanatory variables. Table D.4 in Appendix shows the results for the mean regressions for the determinants of Communication and Math scores based only on household and student characteristics (vectors C and H). By comparing this mean regression with those which include additional explanatory variables and with the median quantile regression, it is clear that vectors C and H are well defined and appear to be robust in all specifications.

4.7 Conclusions

The idea that schooling scores depend on a mixture of family background characteristics, ability and school (institutional) variables is quite clear. Regarding the issue of intergenerational transmission of inequality in the educational system, the most important question would be if and to what extent a better institutional performance of the school service could compensate for problems related to family background.

By providing integral health solutions, minimizing under-nutrition and providing good conditions in the classroom, training teachers (according to their gaps) can impact positively on low and mean learning outcomes, thus contributing to an improved educational quality and breaking cycles of intergenerational transmission of inequality. Increasing learning outcomes for levels above the median only strengthens the transmission of inequality. Consequently, the equality approach should focus on trying to improve the worst scores and our results show that this can be reached at a significant level closing teacher training gaps, improving classroom conditions and improving health and nutrition.

Score inequality can be reduced most efficiently, considering the complete distribution, by increasing scores in lower quintiles. So even if it is true that improving the impact of our selected variables would have a positive effect on scores, we would only reduce inequality if this occurs for low income quantiles, but not for higher ones. If we improve the impact of our institutional variables throughout the complete distribution, inequality might even increase or at least remain the same.

To ask education policies to focus their efforts regarding inequality-reducing measures on lower income quintiles should not be that difficult, given that an important part of students from higher income quantiles are enrolled in private education. Any action taken by public policies to reduce inequality will have a limited impact regarding its possibility to reduce the intergenerational transmission of (welfare) inequality, since family background is a much stronger force in determining inequality in welfare levels. Nevertheless, since parents' education levels are a much stronger determinant regarding levels of welfare inequality, better performing education policies will not have a short term impact. But they can have an important long term impact, not only improving test scores but helping students to reach a higher level of education.

Appendix A

The Basic Model of Decomposition of a Distributional Change

The decomposition of a distributional change essentially consists of contrasting representations of the income-generation process (evaluating differences in estimated parameters) for two different distributions (two points in time) on the one hand, and accounting for changes in the joint distribution of endowments, on the other. Consider that monthly earnings y depend on hourly wages w and monthly hours of work H. Using counterfactual's distributions for hourly wages and working hours, estimates of the contribution to the observed distributional change ΔD between t and t' due to the change in prices β, endowments X, preferences related to working hours λ, residuals ϵ and possibly of all changes taken together may be found through a Oaxaca-Blinder type of decomposition, which can be depicted as:

$$\Delta D = D(w',H') - D(w,H) = D(\beta',X',\epsilon',\lambda') - D(\beta,X,\epsilon,\lambda)$$

This distributional change can be decomposed into price effects $\Delta\beta$, the effect of changing unobservable factors $\Delta\epsilon$ (after having changed prices), changes in endowments ΔX (after having changed prices and unobservable factors) and the effect of changing working hours $\Delta\lambda$ (after having changed all other factors). The change from the distribution of labour income from t to t' can be defined as:

$$\Delta D = [D(\beta',X',\epsilon',\lambda') - D(\beta,X',\epsilon',\lambda')] + [D(\beta,X',\epsilon',\lambda') - D(\beta,X',\epsilon,\lambda')] + [D(\beta,X',\epsilon,\lambda') - D(\beta,X,\epsilon,\lambda')] + [D(\beta,X,\epsilon,\lambda') - D(\beta,X,\epsilon,\lambda)]$$

Simplifying notation:

$$\Delta D = D_{\Delta\beta}(X',\epsilon',\lambda') + D_{\Delta\epsilon}(\beta,X',\lambda') + D_{\Delta X}(\beta,\epsilon,\lambda') + D_{\Delta\lambda}(\beta,X,\epsilon) \quad (1)$$

Equation (1) represents a sequential decomposition of a distributional change between t and t' in price, unobservable factors, endowments and working hours. This equation does not keep final conditions t' constant in all terms on the right hand side (steps for simulations). Nevertheless, with the use of some algebra, this equation can be rewritten as:

$$\Delta D = D_{\Delta\lambda}(\beta',X',\epsilon') + D_{\Delta\beta}(X',\epsilon',\lambda') + D_{\Delta\epsilon}(\beta',X',\lambda') + D_{\Delta X}(\beta,\epsilon,\lambda') + R \quad (2)$$

Where R is the remainder, in other words, R is the distributional change that has not been isolated in this multidimensional space. It is possible to observe that the first three terms on the right side of equation (2) consider t' as the base year. Due to the path dependency property in this decomposition, it is also necessary to calculate all simulated distributions using t as the base year.[119]

Table A.1: Selected characteristics of the Honduran labour force, 1991-2007

	Percentage				Annualized rate of change		
Year / Period	1991	1999	2005	2007	1991-1999	1999-2005	2005-2007
Dependency ratio*							
Household - Country Level	0.66	0.62	0.56	0.54	-0.65	-1.63	-2.16
Household - Rural Areas	0.72	0.69	0.65	0.6	-0.51	-1.05	-4.2
Household - Urban Areas	0.59	0.56	0.48	0.48	-0.53	-2.39	0.00
Employment status							
Country Level							
Wage employment	51.48	53.6	57.18	53.74	0.51	1.11	-3.01
Self-employment	46.67	40.78	39.62	43.27	-1.58	-0.47	4.61
Mixed Activities	1.85	5.62	3.19	2.99	25.47	-7.21	-3.13
Rural Areas							
Wage employment	37.12	42.59	46.94	45.12	1.84	1.7	-1.94
Self-employment	61.23	53.18	50.43	52.56	-1.64	-0.86	2.11
Mixed Activities	1.65	4.24	2.63	2.32	19.62	-6.33	-5.89
Urban Areas							
Wage employment	68.29	64.07	66.6	62.47	-0.77	0.66	-3.1
Self-employment	29.62	29	29.68	33.87	-0.26	0.39	7.06
Mixed Activities	2.09	6.93	3.72	3.66	28.95	-7.72	-0.81
Real wages (Lempiras 1999)							
Country Level	1,829	2,178	2,277	2,418	2.38	0.75	3.1
Rural Areas	1,321	1,432	1,400	1,508	1.05	-0.38	3.88
Urban Areas	2,424	2,887	3,084	3,338	2.39	1.13	4.12

Note: The indicator of age-dependency used in this table relates the number of individuals aged less than 10 and of those aged 65 and over to the population aged 10 to 64.

Source: Authors' calculations based on data from EPHPM I and EPHPM II.

119 See Bourguignon and Ferreira, in the technical chapter of "The Microeconomics of Income Distribution Dynamics in East Asia and Latin America" by Bourguignon et al. (2005). In order to keep initial conditions t constant, we use: $-\Delta D = D_{\Delta\lambda}(\beta, X, \epsilon) + D\Delta\beta X, \epsilon, \lambda + D\Delta\epsilon(\beta, X, \lambda) + D\Delta X(\beta', \epsilon', \lambda) + R$.

Table A.2: Gini coefficient for household per-capita income and monthly earnings

	Household per-capita income			Monthly earnings		
Year / Area	Country	Urban	Rural	Country	Urban	Rural
1991	54.01	51.16	49.81	50.80	49.08	49.15
1992	55.29	50.77	51.80	51.30	49.59	47.85
1993	56.32	53.45	53.23	52.86	52.11	49.58
1994	55.49	52.45	54.18	53.60	51.77	53.43
1995	57.36	51.68	56.99	56.04	52.00	57.34
1996	53.72	48.68	51.50	51.47	49.10	50.56
1997	55.36	50.93	52.22	54.06	51.50	53.13
1998	54.58	48.24	53.93	51.69	47.68	52.87
1999	56.68	50.18	54.45	54.52	49.99	55.13
2001	58.01	50.80	54.56	53.36	48.75	51.94
2002	60.06	52.48	59.72	56.26	50.26	56.10
2004	58.90	50.68	58.72	55.99	49.99	58.02
2005	60.92	52.57	61.43	57.00	49.46	60.88
2006	58.71	51.11	58.40	55.15	48.56	58.11
2007	55.73	49.41	54.15	55.01	49.19	55.88

Note: EPHPM 2003 presents a high degree of measurement errors.

Source: Authors' calculations based on data from EPHPM I and EPHPM II.

Table A.3: Pro-poor growth rates, 1991-2007

	Country level			Urban areas			Rural areas		
Percentile\Period	'91-'99	'99-'05	'05-'07	'91-'99	'99-'05	'05-'07	'91-'99	'99-'05	05-'07
10th percentile	-16.43	0.52	54.2	-6.93	2.07	3.17	-27.96	0.32	79.35
15th percentile	-11.3	-0.19	45.6	-3.04	2.06	5.64	-20.01	-0.78	67.51
20th percentile	-8.37	-0.46	39.96	-0.95	1.95	6.9	-15.68	-1.21	59.28
25th percentile	-6.38	-0.54	35.9	0.29	1.89	7.7	-12.87	-1.44	53.46
30th percentile	-4.93	-0.5	32.72	1.13	1.84	8.19	-10.85	-1.57	49.01
Growth rate (mean)	4.74	2.17	5.46	5.28	2.19	3.83	2.53	1.63	9.53
Growth rate (median)	4.4	0.59	12.98	5.62	1.43	7.47	1.34	-0.93	17.53
Mean perc. growth rate	3.24	0.64	17.82	5.17	1.61	7.15	0.74	-0.76	27.98

Source: Authors' calculations based on EPHPM I and EPHPM II.

Table A.4: Macroeconomic variables, 1990-2007

Year	Trade balance	Current acc. bal.	Terms of trade*	Real exchange rate*	Inflation rate	Real interest rate
	(as % of GDP)					
1990	-2.7	-1.7	78.0	111.2	21.2	-3.42
1991	-3.1	-5.6	83.7	116.8	26.0	-3.30
1992	-4.1	-7.6	79.0	117.9	9.1	11.53
1993	-9.0	-8.9	87.4	127.0	13.6	7.44
1994	-10.0	-10.0	89.1	141.7	28.8	-3.27
1995	-4.4	-5.1	96.3	129.9	24.8	1.66
1996	-5.1	-8.3	89.6	130.1	22.9	5.55
1997	-5.6	-5.8	110.8	119.0	22.2	8.00
1998	-7.7	-2.8	113.4	109.0	11.6	17.08
1999	-15.0	-4.5	106.3	104.6	11.5	16.67
2000	-12.5	-7.2	100.0	100.0	30.8	-3.05
2001	-13.2	-6.3	94.8	97.1	8.0	14.51
2002	-12.5	-3.6	92.0	97.0	5.1	16.70
2003	-14.1	-6.7	88.0	98.5	5.7	14.23
2004	-18.6	-7.7	87.2	100.9	6.4	12.61
2005	-18.5	-3.1	87.2	100.7	7.2	10.77
2006	-21.0	-3.7	83.2	98.3	5.3	11.47
2007	-28.0	-9.0	81.6	98.1	6.7	9.36

Note: *2000=100.

Source: Based on Central Bank of Honduras data.

Table A.5: Percentage contribution of the proximate determinants to inequality changes of the household per-capita income in rural areas, 1991-2007

	ΔGini = 4.6 points 1991-99			ΔGini = 7.0 points 1999-2005				ΔGini = -7.3 points 2005-07				
Determinant	(1)	(2)	(3)	(1)	(2)	(3)	(4)	(1)	(2)	(3)	(4)	(5)
$\Delta_{a \to r}$	-36.01	-36.01	-36.01	8.84	8.84	8.84	8.84	12.25	12.25	12.25	12.25	12.25
Δ_a	-0.56	-0.56	-0.56	-0.93	-0.93	-0.93	-0.93	-2.72	-2.72	-2.72	-2.72	-2.72
Δ_r	136.57			92.09				-109.5				
$\Delta_{o \to t}$		11.08	11.08		1.36	1.36	1.36		-0.87	-0.87	-0.87	-0.87
Δ_o		-23.49	-23.49		-1.33	-1.33			-42.94	-42.94		
Δ_t		148.98			92.06				-65.73			
$\Delta_{u \to w}$			12.39			11.09	11.09			22.89	22.89	22.89
Δ_u			1.83			4.73	4.73			-8.82	-8.82	-8.82
Δ_w			134.76			76.24	76.24			-79.8	-79.8	-79.8
$\Delta_{rem \to nrem}$							13.1				23.7	23.7
Δ_{rem}							-6.09				-53.45	-53.45
Δ_{nrem}							-8.34				-13.18	
$\Delta_{soc \to other}$												11.64
Δ_{soc}												-13.77
Δ_{other}												11.05
ΔTotal	100	100	100	100	100	100	100	-100	-100	-100	-100	-100

Note: Δ_r is decomposed in $\Delta_{o \to t} + \Delta_o + \Delta_t$ as Δ_t in $\Delta_{u \to w} + \Delta_u + \Delta_w$, Δ_o in $\Delta_{rem \to nrem} + \Delta_{rem} + \Delta_{nrem}$ and Δ_{nrem} in $\Delta_{soc \to nsoc} + \Delta_{soc} + \Delta_{nsoc}$.

Source: Authors' calculations based on EPHPM I and EPHPM II.

Table A.6: Percentage contribution of the proximate determinants to inequality changes of the household per-capita income in urban areas, 1991-2007

	ΔGini = -1.0 points 1991-99			ΔGini = 2.4 points 1999-2005				ΔGini = -3.2 points 2005-07				
Determinant	(1)	(2)	(3)	(1)	(2)	(3)	(4)	(1)	(2)	(3)	(4)	(5)
$\Delta_{a\to r}$	45.3	45.3	45.3	10.8	10.8	10.8	10.8	-7.84	-7.84	-7.84	-7.84	-7.84
Δ_a	-3.65	-3.65	-3.65	-9.74	-9.74	-9.74	-9.74	-1.55	-1.55	-1.55	-1.55	-1.55
Δ_r	-141.6			98.91				-90.61				
$\Delta_{o\to t}$		-15.91	-15.91		-1.09	-1.09	-1.09		4.4	4.4	4.4	4.4
Δ_o		-109.3	-109.3		16.3	16.3			-80.0	-80.0		
Δ_t		-16.41			83.73				-14.96			
$\Delta_{u\to w}$			-159.27			5.48	5.48			11.2	11.2	11.2
Δ_u			-12.87			23.1	23.1			-5.8	-5.8	-5.8
Δ_w			155.72			55.1	55.1			-20.4	-20.4	-20.4
$\Delta_{rem\to nrem}$							7.7				4.43	4.43
Δ_{rem}							-11.33				-34.8	-34.8
Δ_{nrem}							19.91				-49.72	
$\Delta_{soc\to other}$												15.53
Δ_{soc}												-16.26
Δ_{other}												-48.99
ΔTotal	100	100	100	100	100	100	100	-100	-100	-100	-100	-100

Note: Δ_r is decomposed in $\Delta_{o\to t} + \Delta_o + \Delta_t$ as Δ_t in $\Delta_{u\to w} + \Delta_u + \Delta_w$, Δ_o in $\Delta_{rem\to nrem} + \Delta_{rem} + \Delta_{nrem}$ and Δ_{nrem} in $\Delta_{soc\to nsoc} + \Delta_{soc} + \Delta_{nsoc}$.

Source: Authors' calculations based on EPHPM I and EPHPM II.

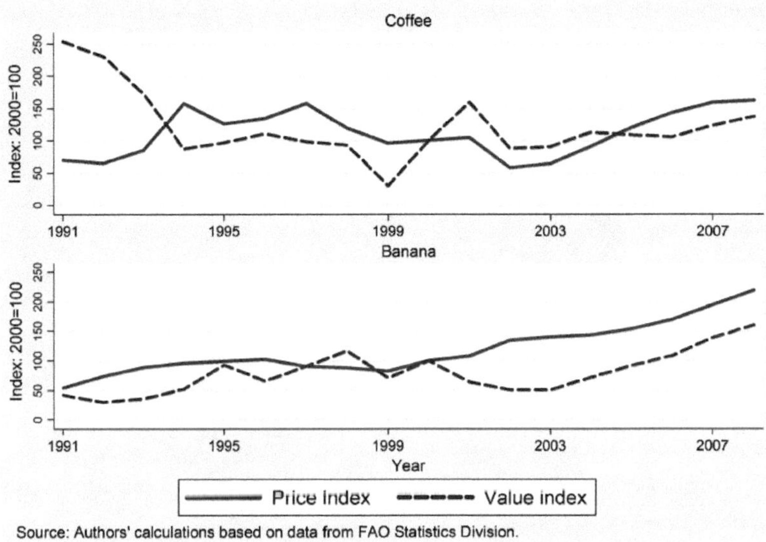

Figure A.1: Principal Honduran export markets, coffee and bananas, 1991-2007

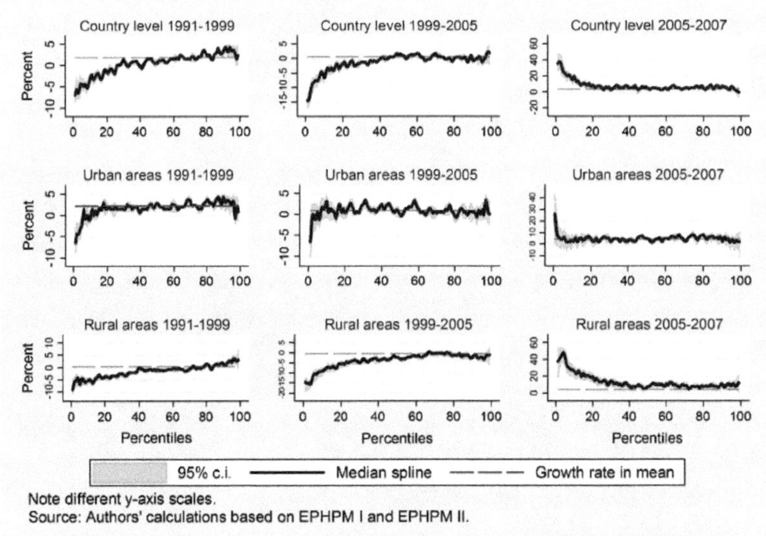

Figure A.2: Growth incidence curves. Monthly labour earnings, 1991-2007

Appendix B

Description of the Simulation Procedure

The simulation procedure aims to avoid the possibility that initial conditions could drive the characteristics of the simulated distributions (i.e. the respective Gini coefficient). In order to achieve this goal, initial parameters' log normal distributions were taken from the observed distribution in Honduras in 1999 and 2005. Table B.1 shows the mean and standard deviation of the log monthly earnings observed in these years according to EPH 1999 and 2005 in real terms.

Table B.1: Distributional moments of the log monthly earnings, 1999 and 2005

	1999		2005	
Distribution	mean	std. dev.	mean	std. dev.
Rural area - tradable sector	6.658	1.076	6.158	1.336
Rural area - non-tradable sector	6.848	1.14	7.115	0.988
Urban areas	7.471	0.988	7.537	1.013

Source: Own elaboration based on data from EPHPM I and EPHPM II.

Using these distributional moments, we proceed to generate a randomly normal distribution of size N=100,000. We truncate each distribution so that the final size of the distribution corresponds to those observed in 1999 and 2005.[120]

However, for the purposes of this simulation, it was necessary to repeat this procedure 100 times. Afterwards, we proceed to replicate tradable, non-tradable and urban distribution 100 times based on underlying populations of size equal to 100,000. Then, by merging tradable and non-tradable distribution it was possible to create rural distributions. Subsequently, by merging rural and urban distribution, we obtained the distributions at the Country level. As a result, this simulation creates 100 rural and 100 country-level distributions. The procedure follows calculating the Gini coefficient for each distribution and bootstrapping them 100 times excluding each time the 10% of the observations. Finally, the reported Gini is the average of the bootstrap Gini coefficients with 100 repetitions. The coefficient of variation of the estimated Gini coefficients does not exceed the 0.5%. In other words, the methodology proves to be effective in making our results independent of the initial conditions.

120 The illustration of these rural distributions can be seen in the right panel of Figure 2.3.

Table B.2: Observed and simulated Gini coefficient using observed distributional moments reported in Table B.1

	Gini coefficient - 1999		Gini coefficient - 2005		Δ Gini	
Distributions	Simulated	Observed	Simulated	Observed	Simulated	Observed
Rural	56.73	55.13	62.4	60.88	5.68	5.75
Country	56.54	54.52	60.29	57	3.75	2.48

Source: Own elaboration based on data from EPHPM I, EPHPM II and random data.

Appendix C

Table C.1: Reduced form of the index function, probit ML. Threshold set at 20,000 inhabitants, 2002-2006 (first step)

Dependent variable: migrant status

	Rural-Urban			Urban-Rural		
Variables \ Model	M1	M2	M3	M1	M2	M3
Basic education	0.356***	0.304***	0.296***	0.0104	0.0769**	0.0757**
Secondary education	0.458***	0.372***	0.317**	-0.0504	0.063	0.0629
Tertiary education	0.573***	0.424**	0.338**	-0.0838*	0.0962*	0.0967*
Potential experience >5 <11	0.097	0.121	-0.0502	-0.0428	-0.0834	-0.0833
Potential experience >10 <16	-0.168	-0.135	-0.327	-0.0755	-0.136*	-0.136*
Potential experience >15	-0.354	-0.342	-0.551**	-0.325***	-0.349***	-0.348***
Avg. household education	-	0.0236	0.0236	-	-0.027***	-0.0262***
$Comm_{ij}$	-2.99***	-3.02***	-5.06***	-	-	-
R_{ab}	1.903***	1.877***	-0.35	-2.653***	-2.637***	-2.966***
Interaction 1	-	-	0.237	-	-	-
Interaction 2	-	-	0.303**	-	-	0.0413
Bi-parental household	0.185**	0.190**	0.225**	0.183***	0.172***	0.171***
Number of Children	0.0128	0.0222	0.0294	-0.0859***	-0.102***	-0.103***
Mapuche	-0.0105	-0.00395	0.0164	0.0026	-0.0121	-0.0148
Female	-0.0104	-0.00918	-0.0122	-0.100***	-0.102***	-0.103***
Unemp. rates at origin	0.0922***	0.092***	0.098***	-0.0270***	-0.027***	-0.027***
Log of population at origin	-0.27***	-0.28***	-0.29***	0.012	0.0201	0.0192
Constant	0.136	0.0477	0.245	-2.344***	-2.234***	-2.229***
Regional controls		Yes			Yes	
Observations		36,115			47,452	
Non-migrant Population		509,549			4,515,090	
Migrant Population		27,285			27,749	
Population Size		536,834			4,542,839	
F	7.524	7.738	7.342	17.74	18.00	17.97
Prob > F	0.0000	0.0000	0.0000	0.0000	0.0000	0.0000

Significance levels: *** p<0.01, ** p<0.05, * p<0.1.

Note: Based on non-enrolled workers 25 years old and older reporting monthly labour earnings in 2006.

Source: Own calculations based on CASEN 2003 and CASEN 2006.

Table C.2: Wage equations adjusted for self-selection. Movers and stayers. Threshold set at 20,000 inhabitants using M2 (second step)

Dependent variable: monthly wages (threshold set at 20,000 inhabitants)

	Rural Origin		Urban Origin	
Variables / Migrant status	Movers	Stayers	Movers	Stayers
Basic education	0.274	0.110***	0.241***	0.138***
Secondary education	0.332	0.268***	0.331***	0.322***
Tertiary education	0.890***	0.537***	0.714***	0.680***
Potential experience >5 <11	0.607**	0.153***	0.0203	0.215***
Potential experience >10 <16	0.526*	0.259***	-0.0029	0.363***
Potential experience >15	0.523**	0.328***	0.118	0.447***
Average household education	-0.0146	0.0382***	0.0420***	0.0374***
Number of children in household	-0.0173	0.0238***	0.0459*	0.0403***
Mapuche	-0.201*	0.0395	0.0963	-0.018
Female	-0.387**	-0.490***	-0.543***	-0.432***
Public sector	-0.0695	0.0583***	0.0474	-0.0225
Rich commune	0.28	-	0.0818	0.271***
Rural sector	0.013	0.0970***	0.0867	-0.0706***
Inverse Mill's ratio (*Lambda*)	-0.0375	0.285***	-0.0181	0.234***
Constant	9.188***	9.188***	9.417***	10.16***
Occupational controls	Yes	Yes	Yes	Yes
Sectoral controls	Yes	Yes	Yes	Yes
Regional controls	Yes	Yes	Yes	Yes
Observations	36115	36115	47452	87304
Population size	536834	536834	4542839	5523250
Censored population	509549	27285	4515090	473621
F	13.71	293	26.07	419.5
Prob > F	0.0000	0.0000	0.0000	0.0000

Significance levels: *** p<0.01, ** p<0.05, * p<0.1.

Note: Based on non-enrolled workers 25 years old and older reporting monthly labour earnings in 2006.

Source: Own calculations based on CASEN 2003 and CASEN 2006.

Table C.3: Structural form of the index function, probit ML, 2002-2006. Threshold set at 20,000 inhabitants using M2 (third step)

Dependent variable: migrant status

	Rural-Urban			Urban-Rural		
Variables	M1	M2	M3	M1	M2	M3
Log-wage differential	3.758***	4.505***	4.592***	3.529***	3.537***	3.537***
Log-wage diff. (sq.)	-0.128	-0.974**	-1.002**	4.48***	4.59***	4.59***
Age	-0.00591*	0.00289	0.00266	-0.008***	-0.008***	-0.0081***
Avg. household educ.	-	0.151***	0.138***	-	-0.0198***	-0.0191***
$Comm_{ij}$	-2.053***	-2.036***	-	-	-	-
R_{ab}	2.126***	1.795***	-	-2.514***	-2.501***	-2.795***
Interaction 1	-	-	-0.185***	-	-	-
Interaction 2	-	-	0.245***	-	-	0.0366
Bi-parental household	0.233**	0.245**	0.261**	0.247***	0.235***	0.235***
Number of children	0.0781	0.156***	0.167***	-0.154***	-0.166***	-0.166***
Mapuche	0.821***	1.121***	1.113***	-0.501***	-0.526***	-0.529***
Female	-0.45***	-0.55***	-0.55***	0.24***	0.24***	0.24***
Unemp. rates at origin	0.082***	0.079***	0.0846***	-0.038***	-0.038***	-0.038***
Log of pop. at origin	-0.376***	-0.477***	-0.48***	0.085***	0.098***	0.097***
Constant	1.432	0.829	0.839	-2.896***	-2.852***	-2.849***
Regional controls		Yes			Yes	
Observations		36,115			47,452	
Non-migrant Population		509,549			4,515,090	
Migrant Population		27,285			27,749	
Population Size		536,834			4,542,839	
F	21.15	30.59	29.41	54.53	51.70	50.30
Prob > F	0.0000	0.0000	0.0000	0.0000	0.0000	0.0000

Significance levels: *** p<0.01, ** p<0.05, * p<0.1.

Note: Based on non-enrolled workers 25 years old and older reporting monthly labour earnings in 2006.

Source: Own calculations based on CASEN 2003 and CASEN 2006.

Table C.4: Structural form of the index function, probit ML, 2002-2006. Threshold set at 40,000 inhabitants using M2 and allowing unemployment (third step)

Dependent variable: migrant status

	Rural-Urban			Urban-Rural		
Variables	M1	M2	M3	M1	M2	M3
Log-wage differential	0.725***	1.210***	1.265***	3.380***	3.792***	3.792***
Log-wage diff. (sq.)	1.237***	0.769***	0.715***	3.988***	4.119***	4.119***
Age	-0.02***	-0.021***	-0.022***	-0.013***	-0.012***	-0.012***
Avg. household educ.	-	0.109***	0.106***	-	-0.049***	-0.0480***
$Comm_{ij}$	-2.66***	-2.608***	-	-	-	-
R_{ab}	2.159***	2.000***	-	-2.948***	-2.917***	-3.12***
Interaction 1	-	-	-0.23***	-	-	-
Interaction 2	-	-	0.24***	-	-	0.0241
Bi-parental household	0.298***	0.344***	0.356***	0.282***	0.253***	0.252***
Number of children	-0.0263	0.0327	0.0386	-0.207***	-0.255***	-0.256***
Mapuche	0.0117	0.146	0.134	-0.199***	-0.285***	-0.287***
Female	-0.131**	-0.213***	-0.210***	0.233***	0.305***	0.306***
Unemp. rates at origin	0.089***	0.088***	0.088***	-0.056***	-0.061***	-0.061***
Log of pop. at origin	-0.160**	-0.231***	-0.230***	0.0566	0.0896**	0.0890**
Constant	-0.377	-0.737	-0.748	-1.801***	-1.635***	-1.635***
Regional controls		Yes			Yes	
Observations		53,005			33,818	
Non-migrant Population		1,044,193			4,236,425	
Migrant Population		45,008			50,028	
Population Size		1,089,201			4,286,453	
F	16.56	17.30	18.91	42.20	40.38	38.78
Prob > F	0.0000	0.0000	0.0000	0.0000	0.0000	0.0000

Significance levels: *** p<0.01, ** p<0.05, * p<0.1.

Note: Based on non-enrolled workers 25 years old and older reporting monthly labour earnings in 2006.

Source: Own calculations based on CASEN 2003 and CASEN 2006.

Appendix D

Table D.1: Descriptive quantiles, Mathematics scores

Variable / Quantile	1	2	3	4	5
Mathematics score	7.55	13.01	18.02	22.54	26.65
Father with up to secondary education (%)	0.54	0.54	0.57	0.6	0.58
Mother with up to secondary education (%)	0.52	0.54	0.57	0.59	0.56
Father with up to tertiary education (%)	0.05	0.06	0.05	0.05	0.07
Mother with up to tertiary education (%)	0.04	0.06	0.05	0.07	0.08
Good classroom conditions (%)	0.84	0.88	0.9	0.91	0.94
Urban area (%)	0.47	0.53	0.53	0.47	0.44
Never failed to be promoted (%)	0.49	0.57	0.63	0.66	0.68
Illness rate < 11 years, last 90 days (%)	0.56	0.56	0.55	0.54	0.56
Health insurance rate < 11 years (%)	0.19	0.2	0.21	0.21	0.21
Teacher speaks usually Spanish (%)	0.81	0.86	0.88	0.9	0.92
Family only speaks Guaraní (%)	0.33	0.31	0.31	0.36	0.38
Frequently works for money (%)	0.37	0.31	0.27	0.23	0.19
Frequently absent due to work (%)	0.25	0.2	0.17	0.17	0.15
Low or moderate absence rates (%)	0.52	0.61	0.66	0.68	0.72
Population - extreme poverty (%-district mean)	0.14	0.15	0.15	0.16	0.17
Population - poverty (%-district mean)	0.32	0.33	0.33	0.34	0.34
Stunting risk (%-district mean)	0.24	0.23	0.24	0.24	0.26
Stunting (%-district mean)	0.11	0.12	0.12	0.12	0.13
Starving risk (%-district mean)	0.19	0.18	0.18	0.18	0.19
Starving (%-district mean)	0.09	0.09	0.09	0.09	0.08

Source: Joint database EPH 2005 (DGEEC), SNEPE 2003 (MEC), WEI-SPS 2006 (UNESCO).

Table D.2: Descriptive quantiles, Communication score

Variable / Quantile	1	2	3	4	5
Communication score	6.37	10.54	13.95	17.41	22.1
Father with up to secondary education (%)	0.57	0.57	0.56	0.57	0.57
Mother with up to secondary education (%)	0.56	0.57	0.56	0.54	0.55
Father with up to tertiary education (%)	0.04	0.05	0.06	0.06	0.07
Mother with up to tertiary education (%)	0.04	0.05	0.06	0.06	0.09
Good classroom conditions (%)	0.85	0.87	0.9	0.93	0.93
Urban area (%)	0.42	0.48	0.55	0.53	0.46
Never failed to be promoted (%)	0.49	0.55	0.64	0.68	0.68
Illness rate < 11 years, last 90 days (%)	0.56	0.56	0.56	0.54	0.55
Health insurance rate < 11 years (%)	0.18	0.2	0.23	0.22	0.2
Teacher speaks usually Spanish (%)	0.8	0.86	0.88	0.9	0.93
Family only speaks Guaraní (%)	0.39	0.35	0.28	0.32	0.36
Frequently do paid work (%)	0.36	0.33	0.26	0.22	0.18
Frequently absent due to work (%)	0.25	0.21	0.17	0.15	0.16
Low or moderate absence rates (%)	0.55	0.61	0.65	0.67	0.71
Pop. in extreme poverty (% - district mean)	0.14	0.15	0.15	0.15	0.18
Population in poverty (% - district mean)	0.31	0.33	0.34	0.34	0.35
Stunting risk (% - district mean)	0.24	0.23	0.23	0.24	0.25
Stunting (% - district mean)	0.12	0.12	0.12	0.11	0.13
Starving risk (% - district mean)	0.19	0.18	0.18	0.18	0.19
Starving (% - district mean)	0.09	0.09	0.09	0.09	0.09

Source: Joint database EPH 2005 (DGEEC), SNEPE 2003 (MEC), WEI-SPS 2006 (UNESCO).

Table D.3: Descriptive schooling statistics

Official school age (years)	Graduation age	Duration
Pre-school, 2005	5	3
Primary school, 2005	11	6
Secondary school, 2005	17	6
Compulsory education, 2005	14	9
Population (1,000)	**Male**	**Female**
Pre-school age, 2006	221	213
Primary school age, 2006	429	415
Secondary school age, 2006	408	395
Total population, all ages, 2007	3096	3031
Net enrolment ratio (%)		
Pre-school NER, 2004	29.5	30.4
Primary school NER, 2004	93.6	94
Secondary school NER, 1991	25.6	27
Gross enrolment ratio (%)		
Pre-school GER, 2004	34.1	34.5
Primary school GER, 2004	113.4	109.9
Secondary school GER, 2004	66	67.3
Entrance and transition (%)		
Primary net intake rate, 1991	72.8	71.4
Primary gross intake rate, 2004	117.2	114.3
Primary entrants with ECCE, 2004	74	76.4
Transition rate primary-secondary, 2003	90.3	90.3
Repetition and completion		
Primary repetition rate (%), 2004	7.9	5.4
Secondary repetition rate (%), 2004	1.2	0.6
Survival rate to grade 5 (%), 2003	79.4	83.3
Survival rate to last primary grade (%), 2003	74.4	78.7
Primary completion rate (%), 2004	93.6	95.3
School life expectancy (years), 2004	10.9	10.7
Total public expenditure on education		
As % of GDP, 2003	4.7	
As % of total government expenditure, 2003	11	

Sources: United Nations Population Division, World Population Prospects: The 2006 Revision, March 2007.
UNESCO Institute for Statistics, January 2008.
http://stats.uis.unesco.org/unesco/ReportFolders/ReportFolders.aspx.

Table D.4: Baseline OLS regressions. Mathematics and communication test scores, only individual and household characteristics

	Mathematics		Communication	
Variable	Coefficient	std. Dev.	Coefficient	std. Dev.
Age	-0.0489	0.0903	-0.1393	0.0765
Female	0.0343	0.1567	0.2895**	0.127
Perspectives	0.3837*	0.2137	0.6413	0.1605
Secondary Education Father	0.5816***	0.2187	0.3426**	0.1587
Secondary Education Mother	0.3278	0.2074	0.0515	0.1648
College Education Father	0.0673	0.4047	0.6789**	0.2834
College Education Mother	1.1249**	0.3649	0.4409	0.2886
Parents and Homework	1.3131***	0.2494	1.1158***	0.1958
Parents as co educators	1.5672***	0.4189	0.8424**	0.3414
Family language Guaraní	0.9247***	0.2928	0.3003	0.2555
Media	0.9263***	0.1234	0.7751***	0.0921
Brother/Sister look after	-0.9606***	0.2726	-0.7655***	0.216
Constant	14.4317***	0.9844	12.7322***	0.8113
N	9.655		9.655	
Population Size	120,670		116,145	
R^2	0.079		0.065	
F	9.21		10.63	

Significance levels: *** p<0.01, ** p<0.05, * p<0.1.

Source: Own estimates based on joint database EPH 2005 (DGEEC), SNEPE 2003 (MEC), WEI SPS 2006 (UNESCO).

Table D.5: Complete OLS regressions. Mathematics and communication test scores

	Mathematics		Communication	
Variable	Coefficient	std. Dev.	Coefficient	std. Dev.
Age	-0.0001	0.0889	-0.0837	0.0723
Female	-0.145	0.1574	0.1634	0.1279
Perspectives	0.3981*	0.2134	0.633***	0.1607
Paid Work	-0.799***	0.2552	-0.4069**	0.1882
Unpaid Work	-1.3013***	0.2182	-1.1442***	0.1672
Secondary Education Father	0.4983**	0.214	0.327**	0.1554
Secondary Education Mother	0.1458	0.2091	-0.042	0.1659
College Education Father	0.0574	0.3875	0.6636**	0.2779
College Education Mother	1.0822***	0.3532	0.3311	0.2705
Parents and Homework	0.9426***	0.2429	0.8589***	0.1922
Parents as co educators	1.4883***	0.4055	0.788**	0.3424
Family language - Guaraní	0.7621***	0.2914	0.2751	0.2522
Media	0.738***	0.1104	0.6185***	0.0864
Brother / Sister look after	-0.8708***	0.268	-0.6818***	0.2127
Urban area	-0.2817	0.503	-0.0072	0.4222
Public sector	-0.591	0.5572	-0.8196*	0.4412
District health insurance rate	2.1826*	1.1345	0.554	0.8475
District sickness rate	-4.0249**	1.5734	-3.8469***	1.3201
District malnutrition rate	-5.5158**	2.6295	-2.8985	2.107
School Language	1.2945***	0.4131	1.0687***	0.3399
Classroom conditions	1.4993***	0.3928	0.9436***	0.3113
Small school	1.1765***	0.5038	0.4379	0.4323
Alto Paraná	-2.5122***	0.7673	-1.8693***	0.5929
Caazapá	2.62***	1.062	1.2282	1.0663
Canindeyú	3.8905***	1.3961	2.2325*	1.2831
Concepción	-1.8352*	0.998	-1.7225**	0.7974
Cordillera	-3.4031***	0.7658	-1.7909***	0.6714
Misiones	-1.9002*	1.0966	-1.1124	0.7932
Paraguarí	1.2318	0.8359	0.703	0.8617
Constant	15.6073***	1.6811	14.3255***	1.3302
N	9.444		9.444	
Population Size	119,850		115,286	
R^2	0.895		0.976	
F	9.31		9.69	

Significance levels: *** p<0.01, ** p<0.05, * p<0.1.

Source: Own estimates based on joint database EPH 2005 (DGEEC), SNEPE 2003 (MEC), WEI SPS 2006 (UNESCO).

Table D.6: Quantile Regression, dependent variable: Mathematics scores

Variable	Q(0.1)	Q(0.25)	Median	Q(0.75)	Q(0.9)
Age	-0.11795	-0.06398	-0.02463	0.0658	0.0348
Female	0.08544	0.01587	-0.32642	-0.29627	-0.35571**
Perspectives	0.30428	0.04793	0.58662**	0.42608**	0.10436
Paid Work	-0.823***	-1.0185***	-1.060***	-0.666***	-0.38651*
Unpaid Work	-1.149***	-1.742***	-1.7***	-1.093***	-0.9439***
Secondary Education Father	0.8463***	0.9744***	0.644**	0.24883	0.10963
Secondary Education Mother	0.04949	0.28055	0.18983	-0.1551	-0.02582
College Education Father	0.07386	0.40913	-0.12261	0.06102	0.01331
College Education Mother	0.60621	0.92914	1.33207**	0.80413**	0.65121**
Parents and Homework	0.38122	1.09165***	1.46262***	0.79098***	0.35884**
Parents as co educators	1.0703**	1.86552***	1.97967***	1.02659**	0.69359**
Family language - Guaraní	0.21789	0.62825**	1.16788***	0.8589***	0.3184*
Media	0.44829***	0.80482***	1.10758***	0.7666***	0.36665***
Brother / Sister look after	-0.8226***	-1.03402***	-1.4034***	-0.7638***	-0.28006*
Urban area	0.04433	-0.09904	-0.46376*	-0.36185	-0.5354***
Public sector	-0.60093*	-0.70235**	-0.38606	-0.34692	-0.4966**
District health insurance rate	2.44264***	2.20781***	1.59737**	1.6645**	1.3349***
District sickness rate	-2.9773***	-3.24105***	-5.0807***	-3.2373***	-2.1414***
District malnutrition rate	-3.9**	-7.43097***	-5.1694***	-5.3514***	-3.1362***
School Language	1.03103***	1.33521***	1.68139***	1.18315***	0.932***
Classroom conditions	1.47226***	1.65958***	1.50929***	1.811***	1.21399***
Small school	0.49039	1.28924***	1.88915***	0.994***	0.42288**
Alto Paraná	-2.3732***	-3.44164***	-2.9526***	-1.807***	-1.4043***
Caazapá	2.77513***	3.74649***	2.0866***	2.251***	1.6299***
Canindeyú	5.20881***	6.65209***	3.1254***	3.3719***	2.3093***
Concepción	-1.31932**	-1.94716***	-2.903***	-1.2197***	-0.8397***
Cordillera	-1.8436***	-3.36033***	-4.039***	-3.8549***	-2.8098***
Misiones	-0.85852	-1.65761**	-2.5383***	-1.4122**	-1.2345***
Paraguarí	0.74857	1.20832*	1.6507***	1.289***	0.95563***
Constant	8.0354***	10.298***	15.387***	20.307***	24.923***
Observations	9444	9444	9444	9444	9444
Pseudo R-squared	0.0501	0.0758	0.0803	0.0562	0.0494
Bootstrapped Std. Errors			500 Repetitions		

Significance levels: *** p<0.01, ** p<0.05, * p<0.1.

Source: Own estimates based on joint database EPH 2005 (DGEEC), SNEPE 2003 (MEC), WEI SPS 2006 (UNESCO).

Table D.7: Quantile Regression, dependent variable: Communication scores

Variable	Q(0.1)	Q(0.25)	Median	Q(0.75)	Q(0.9)
Age	-0.16179**	-0.2236***	-0.15387*	0.04318	0.04651
Female	-0.13539	0.0511	0.34497**	0.26096	-0.12669
Perspectives	0.36665**	0.47409***	0.65273***	0.66997***	0.5685***
Paid Work	-0.18208	-0.49329***	-0.6348***	-0.5847**	-0.16699
Unpaid Work	-0.72753**	-1.09133***	-1.2991***	-1.21723***	-1.3724***
Secondary Education Father	0.17423	0.31992*	0.43211**	0.20597	0.11052
Secondary Education Mother	-0.05242	-0.03494	-0.0441	-0.038	0.11865
College Education Father	1.39227***	0.66221**	0.5963	0.28684	0.82713*
College Education Mother	-0.1171	0.31959	0.17408	0.97708*	0.53782
Parents and Homework	0.93685***	0.82595***	1.2292***	0.85354***	0.72083***
Parents as co educators	0.63497**	0.91474***	0.93955**	0.65828*	0.56181
Family language - Guaraní	-0.22217	-0.22806	0.18257	0.69842***	0.90868***
Media	0.42372***	0.56705***	0.75762***	0.63904***	0.60414***
Brother / Sister look after	-0.6022***	-0.72816***	-0.7869***	-0.52098***	-0.39774*
Urban area	0.26103	0.30644**	0.40803**	-0.33521	-0.6416**
Public sector	-1.0856***	-1.09374***	-0.7622***	-0.83005***	-0.37136
District health insurance rate	1.28362**	1.29047***	0.4834	-0.89179	0.38528
District sickness rate	-2.4927***	-3.17164***	-4.6514***	-4.32255***	-4.8576***
District malnutrition rate	-2.33022**	-3.20336***	-3.607***	-1.91072	-3.5774***
School Language	0.90004***	1.14141***	0.89637***	1.42537***	1.09077***
Classroom conditions	0.80664***	0.91849***	1.1247***	0.97401***	0.9166***
Small school	0.29891	0.33063*	1.10705***	0.57353**	-0.45568*
Alto Paraná	-1.4578***	-1.5737***	-2.1536***	-2.13901***	-1.84683***
Caazapá	1.54704***	1.27841***	0.60847	1.6721***	1.66985***
Canindeyú	2.39195**	3.18105***	1.75381***	1.62072**	2.11931**
Concepción	-0.47656	-1.25528***	-2.3621***	-2.36516***	-1.83***
Cordillera	-0.54142*	-1.0401***	-1.7501***	-2.80425***	-2.6053***
Misiones	-0.20753	-0.73771	-1.535***	-1.05133*	-1.19874*
Paraguarí	0.18046	0.30585	1.00544**	1.07553**	0.79978**
Constant	8.51413***	11.46177***	14.4894***	17.18069***	20.96956***
Observations	9444	9444	9444	9444	9444
Pseudo R-squared	0.0406	0.0565	0.0661	0.0558	0.0503
Bootstrapped Std. Errors			500 Repetitions		

Significance levels: *** p<0.01, ** p<0.05, * p<0.1.

Source: Own estimates based on joint database EPH 2005 (DGEEC), SNEPE 2003 (MEC), WEI SPS 2006 (UNESCO).

Bibliography

Abramitzky, R. (2009). 'The Effect of Redistribution on Migration: Evidence from the Israeli Kibbutz'. *Journal of Public Economics*, 93(3-4): 498-511.

Acemoclu, D., S. Johnson, and J. A. Robinson (2001). 'The Colonial Origins of Comparative Development: An Empirical Investigation'. *The American Economic Review*, 91(5): 1369-1401.

Agosin, M. (2007). 'Trade and Growth: Why Asia Grows Faster than Latin America', In R. Ffrench- Davis, and J. L. Machinea (eds.), *Economic Growth with Equity: Challenges for Latin America*, Palgrave Macmillan, New York.

Altimir, O., L. Beccaria, and M. González Rozada (2000). 'La Evolución de la Distribución del Ingreso Familiar en la Argentina'. Documento de trabajo de la Maestría en Finanzas Públicas Provinciales y Municipales. La Plata: UNLP.

Amemiya, T. (1985). *Advanced Econometrics*. Cambridge, MA: Harvard University Press.

Angrist, J., and D. V. Lavy (1999). 'Using Maimonides. Rule to Estimate the Effect of Class Size on Scholastic Achievement'. *Quarterly Journal of Economics* 114 (2): 533-575.

Aroca, P. (2004). 'Migración Interregional en Chile: Modelos y Resultados 1987-2002'. Notas de Población, CELADE, Santiago de Chile, No. 78.

Barahona, M., and E. Blas (2008). 'Impacto de las Reformas Educativas en el Movimiento Magisterial Hondureño'. Maestría en Ciencias Sociales, FLACSO Programa Centroamericano de Postgrado. Guatemala: Facultad Latinoamericana de Ciencias Sociales.

Barros, R., M. Carvalho, S. Franco, and R. Mendonca (2006). 'Uma Análise das Principais Causas da Queda Recente na Desigualdade de Renda Brasileira'. *Econômica Revista do Programa de Pós- Graduação em Economia da UFF*, 8(1): 117–47.

Bartel, A. P., and F. R. Lichtenberg (1987). 'The Comparative Advantage of Educated Workers in Implementing New Technology'. *The Review of Economics and Statistics*, 69(1): 1-11.

Basu, K. (1984). The Less Developed Economy: A Critique of Contemporary Theory. Oxford: Blackwell.

Beaudreau, B. C. (1990). 'Transport Cost and Regional Wage Differentials: Evidence from Canadian Microdata'. *Canadian Journal of Regional Science*, 13(1).

Becker, G. S. (1962). 'Investment in Human Capital: A Theoretical Analysis'. *Journal of Political Economy*, Supplement, 70: 9-49.

Bednarzik, R. W. (1993). 'Analysis of U.S. Industries Sensitive to International Trade, 1982–1987'. *Monthly Labor Review*, 116:15-31.

Bell, D. (1973). The Coming of Post-Industrial Society: A Venture in Social Forecasting. New York: Basic Books.

Blinder, A. S. (1973). 'Wage Discrimination: Reduced Form and Structural Estimates'. *Journal of Human Resources*, 8(4): 436-55.

Boeke, J. H. (1953). *Economics and Economic Policy of Dual Societies as Exemplified by Indonesia*, New York: International Secretariat, Institute of Pacific Relations.

Boots, B. N., and P. S. Kanaroglou (1988). 'Incorporating the Effects of Spatial Structure in Discrete Choice Models of Migration'. *Journal of Regional Science*, 28(4): 495-509.

Borjas, G. (1987). 'Self-Selection and the Earnings of Immigrants'. *American Economic Review*, 77(4): 531-53.

Borjas, G. (1988). 'Immigration and Self-Selection'. NBER Working Papers 2566, National Bureau of Economic Research.

Bourguignon, F. (1979). 'Decomposable Income Inequality Measures'. *Econometrica*, 47(4): 901-20.

Bourguignon, F., and F. Ferreira (2005). 'Decomposing Changes in the Distribution of Household Incomes: Methodological Aspects'. In F. Bourguignon, F. Ferreira and N. Lustig (eds.), *The Microeconomics of Income Distribution Dynamics in East and Latin America*. Washington, DC: Oxford University Press for the World Bank.

Bourguignon, F., F. Ferreira, and N. Lustig (1998). 'The Microeconomics of Income Distribution Dynamics in East Asia and Latin America'. Washington: IDB-World Bank Research Proposal.

Bourguignon, F., F. Ferreira, and N. Lustig (eds.), (2005). *The Microeconomics of Income Distribution Dynamics in East Asia and Latin America*. Washington, DC: Oxford University Press for the World Bank.

Bourguignon, F., M. Fournier, and M. Gurgand (2001). 'Fast Development with a Stable Income Distribution: Taiwan, 1979-94'. *Review of Income and Wealth*, 47(2): 139-63.

Brücker, H., and E. Jahn (2008). 'Migration and the Wage Curve: A Structural Approach to Measure the Wage and Employment Effects of Migration'. IZA Discussion Papers 3423, Institute for the Study of Labor.

Brücker, H., and P. Trübswetter (2007). 'Do the Best Go West? An Analysis of the Self-Selection of Employed East-West Migrants in Germany'. *Empirica*, 34(4): 371-395.

Brücker, H., and C. Defoort (2007). 'Inequality and the (Self-)Selection of International Migrants: Theory and Novel Evidence'. IAB Discussion Paper 26.

Busso, G. (2006). 'Migración Interna y Proceso de Desarrollo en el Cono Sur Latinoamericano. Análisis Comparativo e Implicancias de Política en el Periodo 1985-2005 en los Casos de Argentina Brasil y Chile'. Guadalajara, México: II Congreso de la ALAP.

Cardemil, L., J. Di Tata, and F. Frantischek (2000). 'Central America: Adjustment and Reforms in the 1990s'. *Finance & Development*, 37: 34–7.

Case, A., and A. Deaton (1999). 'School Inputs and Educational Outcomes in South Africa'. *Quarterly Journal of Economics* 114 (3): 1047-1084.

CASEN 2003 and CASEN 2006 (Encuesta Nacional de Caracterización Socio-económica) (n.d) Household surveys. MIDEPLAN: Ministerio de Planificación, Gobierno de Chile.

Central Bank of Honduras (2010). Memoria Annual 2009. Tegucigalpa: BCH.

Cobb-Clark, D. A. (1993). 'Immigrant Selectivity and Wages: The Evidence for Women'. *American Economic Review*, 83(4): 986-93.

Coeymans, J. E. (1983). 'Determinantes de la Migración Rural-Urbana en Chile, Según Origen y Destino'. *Latin American Journal of Economics*, formerly Cuadernos de Economía, 20(59):43-64.

Cohen, Y., and Y. Haberfeld (2007). 'Self-Selection and Earning Assimilation: Immigrants from the Former Soviet Union in Israel and the US'. Demography 44: 649-668.

Cornia, G. A., S. Rosignoli, and L. Tiberti (2008). 'Globalization and Health, Impact Pathways and Recent Evidence' WIDER Working Paper 2008/74. Helsinki: UNU-WIDER.

Cornia, G. A. (2012). 'Inequality Trends and their Determinants Latin America over 1990-2010'. WIDER Working Paper 2012/09. Helsinki: UNU-WIDER.

Cowell, F. A. (1980). 'On the Structure of Additive Inequality Measures'. Review of Economic Studies, 47: 521-31.

Cragg, M., and M. Eppelbaum (1996). 'Why has Wage Dispersion Grown in Mexico? Is it the Incidence of Reforms or the Growing Demand for Skills?'. *Journal of Development Economics*, 51(1): 99-116.

Cuervo González, M. (2003). 'Evolución Reciente de las Disparidades Económicas Territoriales en América Latina: Estado del Arte, Recomendaciones de Política y Perspectivas de Investigación'. (LC/L.2018-P). CEPAL. Santiago de Chile.

Damill, M., and R. Frenkel (2012). 'Macroeconomic Policies, Growth, Employment, and Inequality in Latin America'. WIDER Working Paper 2012/23. Helsinki: UNU-WIDER.

Devillanova, C., M. Di Maio, and P. Vertova (2010). 'Labour Mobility and the Redistributive Effects of Trade Integration'. *Economic Journal*, 100: 95-115

DGEEC (2000). 'Perfil Educativo de la Población en Edad de Trabajar'. Asunción, Paraguay: Dirección General de Estadística, Encuestas y Censos.

ECLAC (1999). 'Honduras: Assessment of the Damage Caused by Hurricane Mitch, 1998. Implications for Economic and Social Development and for the Environment'. Available at: http://www.gfdrr.org/sites/gfdrr.org/files/dldocs/%281998%29Hurricane%20Mitch,%20Hoduras%20%28ENG%29.pdf

Efron, B., and R. J. Tibshirani (1993). *An Introduction to the Bootstrap*. New York: Chapman & Hall.

Elizaga, J. C. (1970). 'Migraciones a las Áreas Metropolitanas de América Latina'. CELADE.

EPH 1992 and 2005 (Encuesta Permanente de Hogares) (n.d) Household Surveys. Asunción, Paraguay: Dirección General de Estadísticas, Encuestas y Censos.

EPHPM I and EPHPM II (Encuesta Permanente de Hogares) (n.d.) Household surveys. Tegucigalpa, Honduras: Instituto Nacional de Estadística.

Fafchamps, M., and F. Shilpi (2008). 'Determinants of Choice of Migration Destination'. Policy Research Working Paper Series 4728, The World Bank.

Ffrench-Davis R. (2011). 'Macroeconomy for Decent Work in Latin America and the Caribbean'. Employment Working Paper 79. Geneva: ILO.

Ferreira, F., and R. Paes de Barros (1998). 'Climbing a Moving Mountain: Explaining the Decline of Income Inequality in Brazil from 1976 to 1996'. Washington, DC: Inter-American Development Bank. Mimeo.

Frankfurt, H. (1987). 'Equality as a Moral Ideal'. *Ethics*, 98: 21-43.

Fuller, B., and P. Clarke (1994). 'Raising School Effects While Ignoring Culture, Local Condition and the Influence of Classroom Tools, Rules, and Pedagogy'. *Review of Educational Research*, 64(1): 119-157.

Gasparini, L., and G. Cruces (2010). 'A Distribution in Motion: The Case of Argentina'. In L. F. López-Calva and N. Lustig (eds.), *Declining Inequality in Latin America. A Decade of Progress?* Washington, DC: Brookings Institution Press and UNDP.

Gasparini, L., M. Marchionni, and W. Sosa Escudero (2005). 'Characterization of Inequality Changes through Microeconometric Decompositions: The Case of Greater Buenos Aires'. In F. Bourguignon, F. Ferreira, and N. Lustig (eds.), *The Microeconomics of Income Distribution Dynamics in East Asia and Latin America*. New York: Oxford University Press for the World Bank, 47-82.

Glewwe, Paul (2002). 'Schools and Skills in Developing Countries: Education Policies and Socioeconomic Outcomes'. *Journal of Economic Literature* 40 (2): 436-482.

Glewwe, P., and M. Kremer (2006). 'Schools, Teachers, and Education Outcomes in Developing Countries', *Handbook of the Economics of Education*, Elsevier.

Goldfeld, S., and R. Quandt (1973). 'The Estimation of Structural Shifts by Switching Regressions'. *Annals of Economic and Social Measurement*, 2(4): 475-85.

Greenwood, M. J. (1975). 'Research on Internal Migration in the United States: A Survey'. *Journal of Economic Literature*, 13(2): 397-433.

Greenwood, M. J. (1993). 'Migration: A Review'. *Regional Studies* 27:4.

Greenwood, M. J. (1995). 'Internal Migration in Developed Countries'. In M.R. Resenzweig and O. Stark (eds.), *Handbook of Families and Population Economics,* Amsterdam, North-Holland.

Gujarati, D. (2003). *Basic Econometrics*. 4th ed. Boston: McGraw-Hill.

Hanushek, E. A. (1986). 'The Economics of Schooling: Production and Efficiency in Public Schools'. *Journal of Economic Literature* 24 (3): 1141-1177.

Hanushek, E. A. (1997). 'Assessing the Effects of School Resources on Student Performance: An Update', *Educational Evaluation and Policy Analysis* 19(2):141–164.

Hanushek, E. A. (2002). 'Publicly Provided Education', Handbook of Public Economics, in: A. J. Auerbach, and M. Feldstein (eds.), *Handbook of Public Economics*, edition 1, volume 4, chapter 30, pages 2045-2141 Elsevier.

Harris, J., and M. Todaro (1970). 'Migration, Unemployment, and Development: A Two-Sector Analysis'. *American Economic Review*, 60: 126-42.

Heckman, J. (1974). 'Shadow Prices, Market Wages, and Labour Supply'. *Econometrica*, 42(4): 679-94.

Heckman, J. (1979). 'Sample Selection Bias as a Specification Error'. *Econometrica*, 47: 153-161.

Helwing, R.T. (2001). 'Worker Displacement in a Strong Labor Market'. *Monthly Labor Review*, 124(6):13-28.

Herrick, B. H. (1965). Urban Migration and Economic Development in Chile, (Ph.D. Thesis M.I.T.).

Hoxby, C. M. (2000). 'The Effects of Class Size on Student Achievement: New Evidence from Population Variation'. *Quarterly Journal of Economics* 115 (4): 1239-1285.

Jaramillo, M., and J. Saavedra (2010). 'Inequality in Post-Structural Reform Peru: The Role of Market Forces and Public Policy'. In L. F. López-Calva and N. Lustig (eds.), *Declining Inequality in Latin America. A Decade of Progress?* Washington, DC: Brookings Institution Press and UNDP.

JICA and Instituto Desarrollo (2004). 'Estudio y análisis del sector educativo en Paraguay', Informe Final, Asunción.

Klasen, S. (2009). 'Determinants of Pro-Poor Growth' in von Braun, J. R. Vargas Hill, and R. Pandy-Lorch (eds.), *The 'Poorest and Hungry'*. Washington DC: International Food Policy Research Institute, 195-202.

Klasen, S., T. Otter, and C. Villalobos Barría (2012). 'The Dynamics of Inequality Change in a Highly Dualistic Economy: Honduras, 1991–2007'. WIDER Working Paper 2012/17. Helsinki: UNU-WIDER.

Knight G., and L. Johnson (1997). 'Developing Output and Price Measures for Australia's Tadable and Non-tradable Sectors'. Working Paper No. 97/1, Australian Bureau of Statistics.

Koenker, R., and G. Bassett (1978). 'Regression Quantiles', *Econometrica*, Vol. 46, No. 1. pp. 33-50.

Koenker, R., and G. Bassett (1982). 'Robust Tests for Heteroscedasticity Based on Regression Quantiles' *Econometrica*, Econometric Society, vol. 50(1), pages 43-61, January.

Kremer, M. (2003). 'Randomized Evaluations of Educational Programs in Developing Countries: Some Lessons' *American Economic Review Papers and Proceedings*, 93(2): 102-115.

Krueger, A. B. (1999). 'Experimental Estimates of Education Production Functions'. *Quarterly Journal of Economics* 114 (2): 497-532.

Krueger, A. B. (2003). 'Economic Considerations and Class Size' *Economic Journal*, Royal Economic Society, vol. 113(485), F34-F63.

Lee, F. (1978). 'Unionism and Wage Rates: A Simultaneous Equation Model with Qualitative and Limited Dependent Variables'. *International Economic Review*, 19: 415-433.

Legovini, A., C. Bouillón, and N. Lustig (2005). 'Can Education Explain Changes in Income Inequality in Mexico?'. In F. Bourguignon, F. Ferreira and N. Lustig (eds.), *The Microeconomics of Income Distribution Dynamics in East and Latin America*. Washington, DC: Oxford University Press for the World Bank.

Levin, H. (1999). 'The Public Private Nexus in Education'. *American Behavioral Scientist*, 43(1): 124-137.

Lewis, W. A. (1954). 'Economic Development with Unlimited Supplies of Labour'. *Manchester School*, 28:139-91.

Lomnitz, L. (1977). *Networks and Marginality: Life in a Mexican Shantytown.* Academic Press, New York.

López-Calva, L. F., and N. Lustig, (2010). 'Explaining the Decline in Inequality in Latin America: Technological Change, Educational Upgrading and Democracy'. In L. F. López-Calva, and N. Lustig (eds.), *Declining Inequality in Latin America. A Decade of Progress?* Washington, DC: Brookings Institution Press and UNDP.

Lugones, G., P. Gutti, and N. Le Clech (2007). 'Indicadores de Capacidades Tecnológicas en América'. CEPAL Serie Estudios y Perspectivas, México, 89.

Lustig, N. (ed.) (1995). *Coping with Austerity: Poverty and Inequality in Latin America.* Washington, DC: Brookings Institution.

Maddala, G. (1983). *Limited-dependent and Qualitative Variables in Econometrics*. Cambridge: Cambridge University Press.

Maddala, G., and F. Nelson (1975). 'Switching Regression Models with Exogenous and Endogenous Switching'. *Proceedings of the American Statistical Association, Business and Economic Statistics Section*, 423-26.

Magnani, E. (2001). 'Risk of Labor Displacement and Cross-industry Labor Mobility'. *Industrial and Labor Relations Review*, 54(3): 593-610.

Massey, D. S. (1990). 'Social Structure, Household Strategies, and the Cumulative Causation of Migration'. *Population Index*, 56 (1): 3-26.

Michaelowa, K. (2001). 'Primary Education Quality in Francophone Sub-Saharan Africa: Determinants of Learning Achievement and Efficiency Considerations'. *World Development*, 29 (10): 1699-1716.

Mincer, J. (1978). 'Family Migration Decisions'. *Journal of Political Economy*, 86(5): 749-73.

Ministry of Finance (n.d.). Dirección General de Inversiones Públicas, Secretaría de Finanzas. Tegucigalpa: Gobierno de Honduras.

Mirrlees, J. A. (1975). 'Pure Theory of Underdeveloped Economies'. In L. G. Reynolds (ed.), *Agriculture in development theory*. New Haven: Yale University Press.

Moore, C. (2008). 'Assessing Honduras CCT Programme PRAF, Programa de Asignación Familiar: Expected and Unexpected Realities'. IPC Country Study Series, 15. Brasilia: International Poverty Centre.

Nelson, R., and E. Phelps (1966). 'Investment in Humans, Technological Diffusion and Economic growth'. *American Economic Review*, 56(1): 69-75.

Oaxaca, R. (1973). 'Male-Female Wage Differentials in Urban Labour Markets'. *International Economic Review*, 14(3): 693-709.

OECD (2002). *Education at a Glance*. OECD Indicators 2002, Paris, France: OECD.

OECD-WEI (2003). Financing Education: Investments and Returns: Analysis of the World Education Indicators 2002. Paris, France: OECD-UNESCO.

Papageorgiou, D., M. Michaely, and A.Choksi (eds.) (1991). *Liberalizing Foreign Trade: Lessons of Experience in the Developing World*. Blackwell, Oxford.

Parrado, E., and M. Cerrutti (2003). 'Labor Migration between Developing Countries: The Case of Paraguay and Argentina'. *International Migration Review*, 37(1): 101-132.

Paz Cafferata, J. (2003). 'Case Study, Honduras in WTO Agreement on Agriculture: The Implementation Experience'. FAO Developing Country Case Studies. Rome: FAO.

Pinto da Cunha, J. M. (2002). 'Urbanización, Redistribución Espacial de la Población y Transformaciones Socioeconómicas en América Latina'. Proyecto Regional de Población 2000-2003, Santiago de Chile: CELADE-División de Población.

PNUD (2003). *Informe Nacional sobre Desarrollo Humano*. Paraguay 2003. Asunción, Paraguay: PNUD-DGEEC.

Raczynsky, D. (1980). 'Educacion y Migración'. CIEPLAN.

Robinson, J. (2010). 'The Political Economy of Redistributive Policies'. In L. López-Calva, and N. Lustig (eds.), *Declining Inequality in Latin America: A Decade of Progress?*, Washington, DC and New York: Brookings Institution Press and UNDP.

Rogers, W. H. (1992). 'sg11: Quantile regression standard errors'. *Stata Technical Bulletin 9*: 16–19. Reprinted in Stata Technical Bulletin Reprints, vol. 2, pp. 133–137.

Roy, A. D. (1951). 'Some Thoughts on the Distribution of Earnings'. *Oxford Economic Papers*, 3: 135-146.

Ruehle A., and K. G. Kulkarni (2011). 'Dutch Disease and the Chilean Copper boom – An Empirical Analysis'. *Int. J. Education Economics and DeveBlopment*, 2(1): 61-79.

Schiefelbein, E., and J. Brunstein (2003). 'Paraguay. Education and Employment'. Center for Internacional Studies (CIS) University of Toronto and Centro de Análisis de la Economía Paraguaya (CADEP).

Schiefelbein, E., and N. McGinn (1980). 'How Educational Statistics Can be Utilized for Policy Analysis'. In G. Lewis (ed.), *Data Analysis for educational Planning*, Harvard University.

Schwartz, A. (1973). 'Interpreting the Effects of Distance on Migration'. *Journal of Political Economy*, 81(5): 1153-70.

Sen, A. K. (1997) 'From Income Inequality to Economic Inequality'. *Southern Economic Journal*, 64(2): 384-401.

SENAEH (n.d.). Honduran Secretary for Labour. Tegucigalpa: Honduras.

Shorrocks, A. (1980). 'The Class of Additively Decomposable Inequality Measures'. *Econométrica*, 48(3): 613-25.

Sjaastad, L. (1962). 'The Costs and Returns of Human Migration'. *The Journal of Political Economy*, 70(5), Part 2: 80-93.

SNEPE (1999). *Resultado de las Pruebas Nacionales, Sexto Curso, Informe SNEPE 1999*. Servicio Nacional de Evaluación del Proceso Educativo, Ministerio de Educación. Asunción, Paraguay.

Soto, R., and A. Torche (2004). 'Spatial Inequality, Migration and Economic Growth in Chile'. *Cuadernos de Economía*, Santiago, 41(124).

Stark, O. (1993). *The Migration of Labour*. Cambridge: Blackwell.

Stark, O., and D. Bloom (1985). 'The New Economics of Labor Migration'. The *American Economic Review*, 75(2): 173-78.

Tilly, C., and C. H. Brown (1967). 'On Uprooting, Kinship, and Auspices of Migration'. *International Journal of Comparative Sociology*, 8(2): 139-164.

Todaro, M. P. (1969). 'A Model of Labor Migration and Urban Unemployment in LDCs'. *American Economic Review* 59: 138-148.

Todaro, M. P. (1976). 'Internal Migration in Developing Countries: A Review of Theory, Evidence, Methodology and Research Priorities'. Geneva: ILO.

Tomkins, J. M., and J. Twomey (2000). 'Occupational Mobility in England'. *Applied Economics*, 32(2): 193-209.

Tsegai, D. W. (2007). 'Migration as a Household Decision: What Are the Roles of Income differences? Insights from the Volta Basin of Ghana'. *The European Journal of Development Research*. 19(2): 305-326.

United Nations Department of Economic and Social Affairs Population Division (2000). *World Population Prospects: The 2000 revision*. New York.

United Nations Department of Economic and Social Affairs Population Division (2006). *World Population Prospects: The 2006 revision*. New York.

UNESCO (2008). *A View Inside Primary Schools, A World Education Indicators (WEI) Cross-national Study*, Montreal, Canada: UNESCO Institute for Statistics.

UNESCO-OREALC (2001). *Situación Educativa de América Latina y el Caribe, 1980-2000*. Santiago de Chile: UNESCO-OREALC.

Villalobos Barría, C. (2012). 'Internal Migration and its Impact on Reducing Inter-communal Disparities in Chile', IAI Discussion Papers 220, Ibero-America Institute for Economic Research.

Wacziarg, R., and J. S. Wallack (2004). 'Trade Liberalization and Intersectoral Labor Movements'. *J Int Econ*, 64(2): 411-439.

West, M. R., and L. Wößmann (2003). 'Which School Systems Sort Weaker Students into Smaller Classes? International Evidence.' Kiel Working Paper 1145. Kiel Institute for World Economics.

Wößmann, L. (2003). 'Educational Production in East Asia: The Impact of Family Background and Schooling Policies on Student Performance.' Kiel Working Paper 1152. Kiel: Institute for World Economics.

Wilkinson, R., and K. Pickett (2010). *The Spirit Level: Why Equality is Better for Everyone*. London: Penguin Books Limited.

Willis, R., and S. Rosen (1979). 'Education and Self-Selection'. *Journal of Political Economy*, 87(5): 7-36.

Wolff, L., E. Schiefelbein, and P. Schiefelbein (2002). 'Primary Education in Latin America: the Unfinished Agenda'. Washington DC: Inter-American Development Bank.

World Bank (2006a). 'Honduras Poverty Assessment: Attaining Poverty Reduction'. WB Report 35622-HN. Washington, DC: World Bank.

World Bank (2006b). 'Honduras Country Brief'. Retrieved 20 June 2007.

World Bank (n.d.). World Development Indicators. Washington, DC: World Bank.

Yashiv, E. (2004). 'The Self-Selection of Migrant Workers Revisted'. IZA Discussion Papers 1094, Institute for the Study of Labor.

Zea-Barriga, H., E. Aninat and E. Cieslikowski (1981). Economic Memorandum on Paraguay, The World Bank, Latin America and the Caribbean Regional Office, Report No. 3569-PA, Washington DC., p. 249.

Göttinger Studien zur Entwicklungsökonomik
Göttingen Studies in Development Economics

Herausgegeben von / Edited by Hermann Sautter
und / and Stephan Klasen

Die Bände 1-8 sind über die Vervuert Verlagsgesellschaft (Frankfurt/M.) zu beziehen.

Bd. / Vol. 9 Hermann Sautter / Rolf Schinke (eds.): Social Justice in a Market Economy. 2001.

Bd. / Vol. 10 Philipp Albert Theodor Kircher: Poverty Reduction Strategies. A comparative study applied to empirical research. 2002.

Bd. / Vol. 11 Matthias Blum: Weltmarktintegration, Wachstum und Innovationsverhalten in Schwellenländern. Eine theoretische Diskussion mit einer Fallstudie über „Argentinien 1990-1999". 2003.

Bd. / Vol. 12 Jan Müller-Scheeßel: Die Privatisierung und Regulierung des Wassersektors. Das Beispiel Buenos Aires / Argentinien. 2003.

Bd. / Vol. 13 Ludger J. Löning: Economic Growth, Biodiversity Conservation, and the Formation of Human Capital in a Developing Country. 2004.

Bd. / Vol. 14 Silke Woltermann: Transitions in Segmented Labor Markets. The Case of Brazil. 2004.

Bd. / Vol. 15 Jörg Stosberg: Political Risk and the Institutional Environment for Foreign Direct Investment in Latin America. An Empirical Analysis with a Case Study on Mexico. 2005.

Bd. / Vol. 16 Derk Bienen: Die politische Ökonomie von Arbeitsmarktreformen in Argentinien. 2005.

Bd. / Vol. 17 Dierk Herzer: Exportdiversifizierung und Wirtschaftswachstum. Das Fallbeispiel Chile. 2006.

Bd. / Vol. 18 Jann Lay: Poverty and Distributional Impact of Economic Policies and External Shocks. Three Case Studies from Latin America Combining Macro and Micro Approaches. 2007.

Bd. / Vol. 19 Kenneth Harttgen: Empirical Analysis of Determinants, Distribution and Dynamics of Poverty. 2007.

Bd. / Vol. 20 Stephan Klasen / Felicitas Nowak-Lehmann: Poverty, Inequality and Migration in Latin America. 2008.

Bd. / Vol. 21 Isabel Günther: Empirical Analysis of Poverty Dynamics. With Case Studies from Sub-Saharan Africa. 2007.

Bd. / Vol. 22 Peter Dung: Malaysia und Indonesien: Wirtschaftliche Entwicklungsstrategien in zwei Vielvölkerstaaten. 2008.

Bd. / Vol. 23 Thomas Otter: Poverty, Income Growth and Inequality in Paraguay During the 1990s. Spatial Aspects, Growth Determinants and Inequality Decomposition. 2008.

Bd. / Vol. 24 Mark Misselhorn: Measurement of Poverty, Undernutrition and Child Mortality. 2008.

Bd. / Vol. 25 Julian Weisbrod: Growth, Poverty and Inequality Dynamics. Four Empirical Essays at the Macro and Micro Level. 2008.

Bd. / Vol. 26 Johannes Gräb: Econometric Analysis in Poverty Research. With Case Studies from Developing Countries. 2009.

Bd. / Vol. 27 Sebastian Vollmer: A Contribution to the Empirics of Economic and Human Development. 2009.

Bd. / Vol. 28 Wokia-azi Ndangle Kumase: Aspects of Poverty and Inequality in Cameroon. 2010.

Bd. / Vol. 29 Adriana Rocío Cardozo Silva: Economic Growth and Poverty Reduction in Colombia. 2010.

Bd. / Vol. 30 Ronald Kröker: Ansätze zur Implementierung von RSE (CSR) in einem lateinamerikanischen Entwicklungsland. Das Beispiel Paraguay – Eine wirtschafts- und unternehmensethische Untersuchung. 2010.

Bd. / Vol. 31 Maria Ziegler: Institutions, Inequality and Development. 2011.

Bd. / Vol. 32 Melanie Grosse: Measurement of Trends in Wellbeing, Poverty, and Inequality with Case Studies from Bolivia and Colombia. 2011.

Bd. / Vol. 33 Boris Branisa Caballero: Social Institutions, Gender Inequality, and Regional Convergence in Developing Countries. 2012.

Bd. / Vol. 34 Mirko Bendig: Empirical Analysis of Participation Patterns in Microfinancial Markets. The Cases of Ghana and Sri Lanka. 2012.

Bd. / Vol. 35 Robert Rudolf: Employment, Well-Being and Gender: Dynamics and Interactions in Emerging Asia. 2012.

Bd. / Vol. 36 Philipp Kolo: New Approaches to the Dynamics, Measurement and Economic Implications of Ethnic Diversity. 2012.

Bd. / Vol. 37 Carlos Villalobos Barría: Economic Inequality in Latin America. Migration, Education and Structural Change. 2013.

www.peterlang.de